Provides not only practical advice for those navigating the waters of racially diverse ministry but also an overview of the place of the multiracial movement in the larger Christian context. These are words that must be heard by all who want to create racially relevant ministries.

—*Dr. George Yancey, University of North Texas*

Gives us all a vision and a charge to continue the hard but rewarding work of multi-ethnic ministry as we overcome the challenges of uniculturalism and racial segregation in church.

—*Dr. David Anderson, Pastor, Bridgeway Community Church, and Author,* Multicultural Ministry and Gracism

By sharing personal experiences and biblical insights, DeYmaz and Li equip and encourage leaders of multi-ethnic churches to overcome obstacles that surely will surface.

—*Bruce Menning*

Ethnic Blends is such an important study for anyone in church leadership.

—*Dr. Darryl DelHousaye, President, Phoenix Seminary*

Tells the stories of pioneering pastors who have taken their church into uncharted territory to become multi-ethnic by reaching all peoples right in their own community, and shares practical examples of how this works itself out.

—*DJ Chuang, Director, Leadership Network*

God called us to reach people, love people, and help people grow in Christ, no matter what their background is. This book helps us to recapture that vision in a powerful way.

—*Jonathan Falwell, Pastor, Thomas Road Baptist Church*

DeYmaz and Li share their vision. But more important, they also spell out for all who want to join them the real-world challenges and the spiritual rewards, as well as the practical steps that can turn the dream into reality.

—*Larry Osborne, Pastor and Author, North Coast Church*

This is one of the few books that help us to figure out, and consequently live out, the multicolored, multifaceted, missional experiment that is the church.

—*Alan Hirsch, Author (www.theforgottenways.org)*

A must-read for helping churches overcome the many obstacles that divide us. I will be requiring the church planters that we train to read this book.

—*Brian Bloye, Lead Pastor, West Ridge Church*

Boldly puts forward an informed pastoral approach to help church planters, pastors, and emerging pioneers diversify their congregations.

—*Gerardo Marti, Sociologist, and Author of* A Mosaic of Believers

Every brave planter who chooses to pursue the Revelation 7 vision of "all people" will benefit from the trail these pioneers have blazed.

—*George Klippenes, Starting Churches Director, Evangelical Free Church*

For those doing the hard and important work of helping to build the ethnically diverse church, *Ethnic Blends* offers much-needed encouragement and a road map forward.

—*Soong-Chan Rah, Author, and Professor, North Park Theological Seminary*

A must-read for those who are serious about the church becoming a taste on earth of what it will be in heaven.

—*Rodney L. Cooper, Professor, Gordon-Conwell Theological Seminary*

If you have ever struggled with the homogenous principle as sociology trumping theology, this book will resonate with you.

—*Eric Geiger, Executive Pastor, Christ Fellowship Miami*

This book is an essential resource for anyone working to build a multi-ethnic church.

—*Major Mary Hammerly, Director of Multicultural Ministries Department, Salvation Army*

An indispensable guide for making diversity a permanent, and thus more authentic, part of our personal and congregational lives.

—*Edward Gilbreath, Editor, UrbanFaith.com, and Author,* Reconciliation Blues

An encyclopedia of multi-ethnic church knowledge developed by two of the best practioners today.

—*Tom Cheyney, Team Leader, Church Planting Group, North American Mission Board*

A Christ-centered road map that offers practical wisdom on how to form multi-ethnic congregations. DeYmaz and Li are redemptive voices crying out in a wilderness of homogeneity for the church in all its ethnic diversity to be one as God is one.

—*Paul Louis Metzger, Professor, Multnomah Biblical Seminary, and Author,* Consuming Jesus: Beyond Race and Class Divisions in a Consumer Church

An excellent and timely book for every Christian who wants to be a part of the multi-ethnic revolution.

—*Chad Brennan, Founder and Director of ReNew Partnerships and TheNewCulture.org*

Lays out a tremendous vision with solid theological reasoning for the purpose of building churches that are ethnically diverse while giving practical suggestions for overcoming the obstacles we face along the way.

—*Dave Ferguson, Lead Pastor, Community Christian Church, and Author,* Exponential

ETHNIC BLENDS

The Leadership Network Innovation Series

The Big Idea: Focus the Message, Multiply the Impact,
Dave Ferguson, Jon Ferguson, and Eric Bramlett

*Confessions of a Reformission Rev.: Hard Lessons from
an Emerging Missional Church,* Mark Driscoll

*Deliberate Simplicity: How the Church Does
More by Doing Less,* Dave Browning

*Leadership from the Inside Out: Examining the Inner
Life of a Healthy Church Leader,* Kevin Harney

*The Monkey and the Fish: Liquid Leadership
for a Third-Culture Church,* Dave Gibbons

*The Multi-Site Church Revolution:
Being One Church in Many Locations,*
Geoff Surratt, Greg Ligon, and Warren Bird

*Servolution: Starting a Church
Revolution through Serving,* Dino Rizzo

Sticky Church, Larry Osborne

Other titles forthcoming

LEADERSHIP NETWORK®
innovation series

ETHNIC BLENDS

Mixing Diversity into Your Local Church

MARK DEYMAZ AND HARRY LI

ZONDERVAN®

ZONDERVAN.com/
AUTHORTRACKER
follow your favorite authors

ZONDERVAN

Ethnic Blends
Copyright © 2010 by Mark DeYmaz

This title is also available as a Zondervan ebook.
Visit www.zondervan.com/ebooks.

This title is also available in a Zondervan audio edition.
Visit www.zondervan.fm.

Requests for information should be addressed to:
Zondervan, *Grand Rapids, Michigan* 49530

Library of Congress Cataloging-in-Publication Data

DeYmaz, Mark, 1961–
        Ethnic blends : mixing diversity into your local church / Mark DeYmaz and
Harry Li.
            p. cm.
        Includes bibliographical references.
        ISBN 978-0-310-32123-1 (softcover)
        1. Church and minorities. 2. Church work with minorities. 3.
    Ethnicity — Religious aspects — Christianity. 4. Multiculturalism — Religious
    aspects — Christianity. I. Li, Harry. II. Title.
    BV639.M56D495 2009
    259.089 — dc22   2009040177

Cover and interior design by Matthew Van Zomeren

Printed in the United States of America

10 11 12 13 14 15 16 • 21 20 19 18 17 16 15 14 13 12 11 10 9 8 7 6 5 4 3 2 1

(MD)
To my wife, Linda,
who gives so much, is thanked so little,
and even so, walks intimately with God.
You are an inspiration to me,
a treasured gift from the Lord above.

(HL)
To my wife, Melanie,
and my children, Anna, Katie, and Meredith.
My home is my shelter, strong tower, and fortress.
Thank you for being such an important part
of my life and calling.
You all have made "walking in the door" each evening
the most eagerly anticipated part of every day.

CONTENTS

FOREWORD
by Erwin Raphael McManus

WITH A NAME LIKE ERWIN MCMANUS, it's probably not that obvious that I'm an immigrant. Less obvious is that I'm from El Salvador and that Spanish is my first language. I came to the States as a child and have spent my life in a cross-cultural world. While I have integrated well enough to seem as if I was born here, it's a mistake to conclude that my experience was anything but one of a stranger in a strange land. I did not escape the sting of discrimination that invariably comes when you are a minority in a majority culture.

When I was a young boy, I was given my alias, which allowed me to better fit into this new world. Though my named was changed, I have never been a member of the majority culture. I have always been an outsider looking in. About five years ago I became a U.S. citizen. I am so grateful. I love this country and all the opportunity it has afforded me and my family. This journey in some ways gives me a unique perspective on the topic this book tackles.

I have seen five decades of change in the U.S. and know both how much progress has been made and how much remains to be made when it comes to issues of diversity, racism, and the need for reconciliation and even restitution. There are many important issues and conversations taking place concerning the cultural and political complexities related to the growing issue of diversity, and beyond that pluralism.

One of the recurring themes in my life has been of bad timing—specifically starting things before their time. If your timing is right, you are in line for great success and popularity. If you're too late, you're just a bandwagoner or an also-ran. If you're too soon, you're a heretic.

It was in the early 1980s when we launched our first experience with a multisite congregation, never realizing that one day the megachurch approach would become so last year and that the trend would move toward this expression of community.

During those same early years, we also began two critical social experiments. The first was to become the first community of faith in the U.S. (so we were told) to reclaim land in an urban center and begin a reversal of white flight and urban decay. We decided to take back the city while everyone's affections were held captive by the allure of massive suburban growth. People thought we were out of our minds and out of touch with what God was doing.

The second was to move toward radical diversity. At that time, the social dynamics were the crisis of black-white tensions, with the added complexity of immigrants from south of the boarder. We had the incredible opportunity of bringing together all three cultures into one community of faith during the church growth movement, in which the homogenous principle was gospel. We did grow more slowly because of our diversity, but it was a price we were willing to pay to create a culture of inclusion.

We were not CEOs looking at the bottom line; we were artists creating something beautiful. We were cultural architects determined to design a future in which faith brought the world together, rather than kept us apart. We were told we were attempting the impossible. It's all about timing. *Possible* simply means present and past tense. *Impossible* is a synonym for in the future. It is waiting on us.

When we named our present community Mosaic, we threw ourselves into the future. When I proposed the name to our elders, they liked it, but said it's not who we were. They forgot the yet. So we chose the name knowing we were not yet a mosaic. It was our future. Our nonnegotiable impossible future.

Today, here in Los Angeles, Mosaic reflects something like seventy different ethnicities. It is as if the world has come together. We have no clear majority, though our Asian population accounts for over 40 percent of our community of faith. Still, when you break it down to Chinese, Japanese, Korean, Filipino, Thai, Indian, Burmese, Indonesian, and a host of other Asian ancestries, there is no majority at all. Mosaic is a sea of diversity.

So when I first met Mark DeYmaz, I felt an instant affinity with him. He has a heart to bring the world together and a burden to call all of us who are followers of Christ to carry this banner. For him Mosaic is more than a name; it is a symbol of hope and a promise of change. We all live in a new world filled with great peril and great opportunity. We live in a world divided and in conflict. The church hasn't been of great service here. We have held the line of demarcation almost as if it were a badge of honor.

Mark is calling us to choose a new way. If we heed this call, we will at last reflect the one whose name we bear. We will be to the world what Jesus has been for us—a source of hope. If we act now, we still have a chance to lead the way. The world is in desperate need of those who will tear down the dividing walls between us and bring us together.

We are already late … but not too late.

Help us bring the mosaic together. You just might be the missing piece.

Join us in this Mosaic revolution.

—Erwin Raphael Mcmanus
Mosaic Global Initiative
Los Angeles

FOREWORD
by Michael Emerson

FOR AT LEAST THE PAST 150 years of American history, churches have managed racial and ethnic diversity by segregating it. That is, separate congregations — and in the case of Protestantism, separate denominations — were formed for people of different racial and ethnic backgrounds. Odd, really. Think of what this says — race and ethnicity, these social creations of humans, are considered so important that churches organize masses of people into separate congregations and denominations.

Let's be blunt about this. Race really is that important in the United States. And this is indeed why churches are racially homogeneous. But Christians are called to bring down dividing walls, not live comfortably behind them.

Ethnic Blends is a vital book for a number of reasons. It moves us beyond those historical dividing walls. What is more, the book and its authors represent what is indeed a new spiritual movement. That movement is saying, "What is biblical is that the diversity of believers ought to be together, *within* congregations." Mark DeYmaz and Harry Li identify changes afoot, and they are correct.

For example, in 1998 a national study of American congregations found that just 5 percent of Protestant churches were racially diverse (no one racial group is 80 percent or more of the congregation). No differences existed between large churches (one thousand or more attenders) and other churches. When this same study was conducted in 2007, a major change was revealed. Large Protestant churches were three times more likely to be multiracial in 2007 than in 1998. And if we focus just on evangelical churches, large congregations were five times more likely in 2007 than in 1998 to be multiracial. This is seismic change in such a short time. These changes have come about due to a spiritual movement that has emerged and is discussed in *Ethnic Blends*. Large churches typically are the bellwether of change to come through-out Christendom. More change, then, is coming. An old system is crumbling, and a new one — the multiracial congregation — is emerging.

And thus we need direction. We need guidance on what challenges to expect, how to address them, how to worship and walk together, how to form community, and how to work for justice. *Ethnic Blends* brings us a giant leap forward on these questions. It provides firsthand accounts and draws on the best of a variety of experiences. The authors discuss a range of obstacles that those engaged in multi-ethnic ministry will inevitably face. Each chapter directly takes on real issues and provides honest, biblically and experientially informed responses. A treasure chest.

The goal is godly. The obstacles to the goal are a certainty. Keep *Ethnic Blends* with you when the obstacles arise, and stay focused on the goal: the Lord's diverse creation worshiping together, working toward a world where we care for each other as God's children.

— Michael O. Emerson, PhD
Allyn and Gladys Cline Professor of Sociology,
and Director, Center on Race, Religion,
and Urban Life, Rice University

ACKNOWLEDGMENTS

(MD): THANKS, GUYS — Zack, Emily, Will, and Kate — for exercising your own measure of faith, courage, and sacrifice through the years as cofounders of Mosaic! I look forward to the day when you more fully comprehend how God has used you to help pioneer a global movement. Harry, I'm so thankful God sent you to me as a faithful friend and colleague. Throughout the past eight years, your encouragement and insight have been invaluable! I'm so thrilled now to share it, and you, with others. Mom, what can I say? Where would I be without your investment of love, time, money, and prayers over these (gulp) nearly fifty years of my life! And to the elders, staff, and people of Mosaic, who daily brew ethnic blends. Thanks for who you are, for all you've become, and for joining Linda and me on the journey. It's truly a privilege to once again represent your commitment to Christ, to one another, and to the multi-ethnic vision in print. Even still, I believe our best is yet to come!

Special thanks to Greg Kappas for reviewing certain sections of this work, for additional theological insights, and for faithful friendship since 1985. That goes for you too, Debbie! And to you guys, as well — Jim Spoonts, George Yancey, and Willie Peterson — for all you have done to advance the movement. To Wayne, Michael, David N., Jonathan, Alex, Ed, Daniel, Chris, Dana, Mont, Efrem, Pete, David A., and David B. — thanks for your friendship, your partnership, and the honor of including you in this project. Erwin, thanks for your words and, together with Eric Bryant, for friendship, partnership, and alignment via Mosaic Alliance, Mosaic Global Initiative, and Mosaix. And Michael (Emerson), thanks for contributing a foreword and for your pioneering scholarship that continues to influence practitioners like me throughout the United States and beyond.

Finally, I want to thank Dave Travis, Linda Stanley, Greg Ligon, Mark Sweeney, and Stephanie Plagens at Leadership Network for their continued faith in me and in the work I so passionately pursue. And to Paul Engle, Ryan Pazdur, and Chris Fann at Zondervan; it was great to work with you on this project! Thanks for a job well done and for making it fun.

(HL): Thanks to the people of Mosaic; you have been wonderful ambassadors for Christ throughout the past nine years. Your willingness to be patient, prayerful, and hopeful together in Christ has encouraged me more than you will ever know, especially as God has transformed me from major geek into a shepherd of his people! You are the most special group of people I have ever known.

Mark, thanks for taking a chance on a guy with no full-time ministry experience, no formal training, and no clue what it would take to become a pastor of this unique church. Your faith and discernment in leading us never ceases to amaze me. And thanks for asking me to contribute to this project. It's been bubbling up for quite a while, and it felt so good to formalize some of these thoughts on paper.

ACQUIRING THE TASTE
An Introduction

> If the kingdom of heaven is not segregated, why on earth
> is the church?

IT's 5:30 A.M. ON A SATURDAY MORNING, and I (Mark) can't sleep. Once again Linda and I are readying a house to sell, something we seem to do every five years or so, given the changing dynamics of our family and a shared love for design. In fact, we've only recently completed the renovation of an old farmhouse from the 1920s — an extreme home-makeover that's taken us almost four years to complete. So yesterday I spent nearly nine hours power washing the siding, the decks, and the white fencing that surrounds the two-acre property, and I'll be at it again today. I could use a good cup of coffee to get me going.

The problem is, I don't drink coffee ... and wouldn't know how to make a cup if I tried!

Somewhere I once read that the secret to a good coffee blend is high-quality beans, brewed with just the right mix of fresh grounds and boiled water over a specific length of time. And while I do not have personal knowledge or experience in pursuit of the perfect blend, I do know that once achieved, its aroma is refreshingly attractive — even to non-coffee-drinkers like me.

When it comes to mixing diversity into the local church, however, I do have knowledge and a good bit of personal experience. Together with my colleague of eight years, Harry Li, I have led our congregation in pursuit of what we sometimes refer to as *ethnic blends* — the intentional mixing of diversity into the local church. With a desire to inspire, guide, and encourage ministry leaders who long to see local churches reflect the unity and diversity of the kingdom of God on earth as it is in heaven, we are writing this book to promote the further development of multi-ethnic churches throughout North America and beyond. For we have seen that the multi-ethnic church, like a good cup of coffee, produces an aroma that is refreshingly attractive — especially to those without Christ in an increasingly diverse and cynical society.

WHY THIS BOOK?

Since the publication of my book *Building a Healthy Multi-ethnic Church* (San Francisco: Jossey-Bass/Leadership Network, 2007), and following other foundational works on the subject at the start of the twenty-first century, including *Divided by Faith* (Oxford: Oxford Univ. Press, 2001), *United by Faith* (New York: Oxford Univ. Press, 2003), *Multicultural Ministry* (Grand Rapids, Mich.: Zondervan, 2004), and *One Body, One Spirit* (Downers Grove, Ill.: InterVarsity Press, 2005), increasing numbers of pastors, professors, reformers, and researchers alike are recognizing that the multi-ethnic church is not only biblical but also critical to the advance of the gospel in the twenty-first century. Yet the passion for such a church must be driven not so much by the pursuit of racial reconciliation as by the need for men and women to be reconciled to God through faith in Jesus Christ. For this reason, I wrote my first book to ensure quality exegesis, sound theology, and principally correct thinking on the matter.

Now, however, with growing numbers embracing the biblical mandate, the seven core commitments, and the evangelistic intentions of a diverse congregation, I am often asked to address roadblocks and barriers to its success. In other words, what are the obstacles and how can they be overcome if church planters, pastors, and reformers are to establish healthy multi-ethnic churches?

MAPPING THE MOVEMENT

Have you ever found yourself in an unfamiliar environment, one in which you needed a map just to figure out exactly where you were or where next you needed to go? In such times, it takes a special kind of map to point us in the right direction. You know the kind — those large displays centrally located in airports and malls (even in some churches!), marked with an *X* alongside three very helpful words: "You Are Here!" Clear understanding of where we are and where we've come from provides the context to discern the way forward. Before moving on, then, let me provide such a map, a context for understanding the multi-ethnic church movement — where it is, where it's come from, and where I believe the future lies.

The Forerunner Stage
Charting the Movement

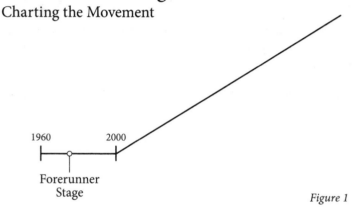

Figure 1

In their book *United by Faith,* authors Curtiss Paul DeYoung, Michael O. Emerson, George Yancey, and Karen Chai Kim present a concise history of the emergence of "multiracial" congregations in the United States in the second half of the twentieth century (the Forerunner Stage). Despite the wonderful leadership of the individuals and churches they cite, church growth and development in those years was primarily governed by something called the *homogeneous unit principle.* In short, this principle suggests that churches grow fastest when they're homogeneous — made up of people from the same ethnic, economic, and educational background. For the most part, the principle is true and can be used quite effectively to build a large church. In other words, target a specific group of people, appeal to their collective wants and wishes, and your church will grow.

The problem with the homogeneous unit principle is that despite the good intentions of those interested in rapidly reaching the world with the gospel (and consequently growing churches quickly), the principle has had the unintended effect of justifying the segregation of local congregations along ethnic and economic lines. The fact is, it has led us even further away from principles and practices that defined New Testament churches such as existed at Antioch and Ephesus — churches in which the love of God for *all* people was clearly on display, churches in which diverse believers learned to walk, work, and worship together as one so the world would know God's love and believe (see John 17:20 – 23ff.; Acts 11:19 – 26; 13:1ff; Eph. 2:11 – 3:6).

Charting the Movement

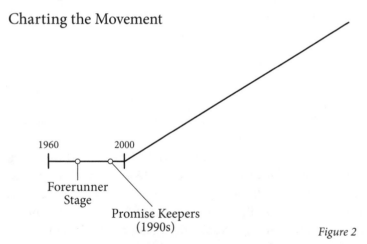

Figure 2

Toward the end of the Forerunner Stage, a new movement called Promise Keepers burst onto the evangelical scene. Among other things, this inspirational effort had the effect of presenting the ideals of "racial reconciliation" in a more palatable way to the conservative evangelical masses. At weekend events, black and white men stood side by side with Latinos and Asians, filling entire stadiums, to sing, study, pray, and even weep together, united by a common faith and their love for Jesus Christ. Yet despite the good feelings that were generated and the well-intentioned efforts of organizers, those who attended would quickly return to the segregated status quo of the congregations from which they came. And the question still remained: Why is such a wonderful expression of unity and diversity not more commonly found within our own local churches and weekly gatherings?

Charting the Movement

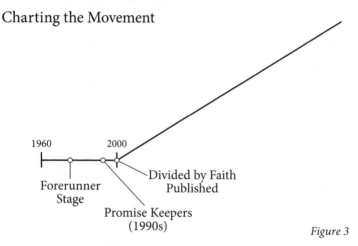

Figure 3

At the start of the twenty-first century, a truly groundbreaking work titled *Divided by Faith* was published. In my mind, this marked the end of the Forerunner Stage and ushered in what I call the Pioneer Stage of the multi-ethnic church movement. Let me tell you why.

For more than one hundred years, it has been widely said that eleven o'clock on Sunday morning is the most segregated hour of the week. However, until *Divided by Faith* was published, the observation remained largely unaddressed. In their book, sociologists Michael O. Emerson and Christian Smith provided statistical data detailing the systemic segregation of the local church throughout the United States. Studying both Catholic and Protestant churches throughout the country at the turn of the century, they showed that 92.5 percent of churches could be classified as "monoracial." This term, they said, describes a church in which 80 percent or more of the individuals who attend are of the same ethnicity or race. The remaining churches (7.5 percent) they described as "multiracial" — churches in which there exists a nonmajority, collective population of at least 20 percent. Using this definition, they determined that approximately 12 percent of Catholic churches, less than 5 percent of evangelical churches, and about 2.5 percent of mainline Protestant churches could be described as multiracial.[1]

Behind the numbers, though, they discovered something far more troubling. Their statistical research confirmed that when compared with other social institutions, the church, far from representing the diversity and unity of the kingdom of God, was actually the primary institution perpetuating systemic (institutional) racism in our society. How, you might ask, is this possible?

Emerson and Smith found that evangelicals spend more than 70 percent of their social time with people from their own congregation. In other words, when people from evangelical churches invite others into their homes, to go out for dinner, or to enjoy a weekend away, most often they invite people who attend their own local church. Since the vast majority of evangelicals attend churches composed of individuals who are similar to them in race and social class, it is unlikely that they (we) have well-developed relationships of transparency and trust with individuals from a different culture. Consequently, most of us in the evangelical church do not really know, nor do we experientially understand the unique challenges faced by the diverse individuals with whom we work, go to school, or share our neighborhood. And since we lack these personal relationships, we are not often motivated to personally involve ourselves in helping to resolve unique challenges associated with their race or culture. Sure, we may be willing to send an occasional check or pray that things will improve, but we are not often willing to commit ourselves to the pursuit of long-term relational development or to invest ourselves in solutions. In light of these findings, the authors suggest that the church continues (unintentionally) to perpetuate systemic racial inequities within society.

By the end of their book, Emerson and Smith effectively argue that the church is a sleeping giant in the effort to dismantle institutional racism in the United States. They propose that one of the best ways to address this systemic problem is to establish multiracial, multi-ethnic churches in which all people are welcome, loved, and cross-culturally engaged. These are churches in which relationships are based upon a genuine love for Christ, in whom members find ways to overcome earthly divides of race and social status. Relationships like these lead to a genuine understanding between people and help us cultivate compassion for others who are not like us. Eventually they lead to a changed society and further the advance of the gospel.

Despite the glowing endorsement the authors give to multi-ethnic congregations, sadly they conclude that we should probably not expect to see many churches like this develop anytime soon, given the all-too-common, more prevalent homogeneous approach to church growth and development.

While some readers were likely discouraged at the bleak prospects for change, many church planters and reformers, like myself and others contributing to this book, were attracted to the challenge and already embracing a new vision for the local church. It was then, I believe, that the multi-ethnic church movement entered the Pioneer Stage.

The Pioneer Stage

Pioneers are usually not the *first* people to discover things. More typically, they are the first to recognize the intrinsic value and significance of something that others have only stumbled upon or taken for granted. Pioneers are the people who risk themselves and their families in pursuit of a dream. They are willing to journey great distances and brave the unknown, endure hardships, persevere in spite of opposition. In time they are the ones who create new realities and change society. Indeed, not only do pioneers see what could and should be; they are blessed with a gift of discernment, seeing what *will be*. Consequently, they devote their time and energy to establish initial forms and functions so that others can more easily follow their lead. In this stage of any movement, pioneers must exercise great faith and courage, and willingly sacrifice themselves to build solid bridges to the future — a future that is not always as clear to others as it is to them.

Charting the Movement

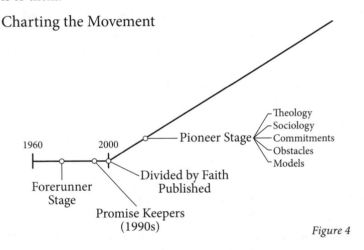

Figure 4

There are several factors that have led me to believe that the multi-ethnic church movement has entered a Pioneer Stage in this first decade of the twenty-first century. One of the initial signs is that an increasing number of books are being published on the subject with each passing year.[2] In addition, multi-ethnic churches (and their leaders) are increasingly the subject of magazine and newspaper articles and are receiving attention on the internet. Indeed, the internet has been a great asset to the movement, fanning the flame through online blogs and newsletters such as *The New Culture*, produced by Chad Brennan of ReNew

Partnerships.[3] You may have also noticed that a growing number of churches are now describing themselves as "multi-ethnic," "multiracial," or "multicultural" on their homepages.

Beyond the emerging signs in print and electronic media, there are now a number of large and well-respected conferences that devote entire tracks of study to the multi-ethnic church and feature plenary speakers who advance the vision. In 2007, 2008, and 2009, for example, the National New Church Conference (now known as Exponential) in Orlando, Florida, hosted both preconference and main conference tracks on the subject, and I expect they will continue to do so well into the future.[4] Likewise, the Ethnic America Network has scheduled similar tracks at their national conferences since 2005.[5] Dave Gibbons, a leading speaker on third-culture leadership and pastor of a multi-ethnic church in Irvine, California, was a main stage speaker in 2008 at Rick Warren's Purpose Driven Network Summit. Also that year, Efrem Smith was featured at Willow Creek's Leadership Summit, and David Anderson was a plenary speaker at the National Outreach Convention — both of them leaders in the multi-ethnic church movement. These friends and fellow pioneers, together with many others, are clearing a trail that will literally change the face of the local church throughout the United States in this century!

Additional evidence that we're in the Pioneer Stage of the movement can be seen in the fact that entire denominations like the Evangelical Covenant Church, the Evangelical Free Church of America, and the Reformed Church in America are now pursuing this vision by hiring staff and creating departments devoted to establishing multi-ethnic churches and pastoral teams. And a growing number of church planters, pastors, reformers, and educators across multiple denominations are now connecting through Mosaix, a network relaunched in 2010 by Erwin McManus and myself, dedicated to catalyzing the multi-ethnic church movement by casting vision, connecting individuals of like mind, conferencing, and coaching.[6]

The Early Adopter Stage
Charting the Movement

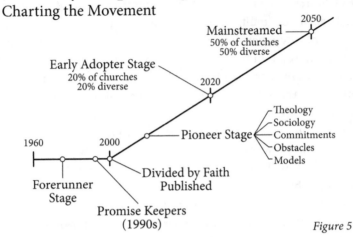

Figure 5

At some point, I believe, the movement will transition from a Pioneer Stage to an Early Adopter Stage. But no one can say for sure when this will happen. My personal hope, and the goal of many of my colleagues within the movement, is that 20 percent of churches throughout the United States will achieve 20 percent diversity by the year 2020. If we are successful in both encouraging and achieving that goal, I believe the movement will be well into the Early Adopter Stage. Following this stage, our belief is that multi-ethnic vision will be embraced by the majority of North American congregations and soon go mainstream. Indeed, our hope and prayer is that we will see 50 percent of churches achieve 50 percent diversity by the year 2050!

This book, then, is being written to help advance these aims and to make it easier for others to get involved in what I believe will be one day viewed as the single greatest movement of God concerning his church in the twenty-first century — namely, its integration for the sake of the gospel.

As I have already noted, I am pleased to partner in this project with my good friend and colleague Harry Li. Harry holds a PhD in electrical engineering, and in 2002 he left a tenured professorship at the University of Idaho to join me and a handful of others (squeezing into four hundred square feet of rented office space) in hopes of building a healthy multi-ethnic church we called the Mosaic Church of Central Arkansas. Believe me, it was quite the step of faith for both him and his family, and I've asked Harry, here, to share more of his story.

INTRODUCING HARRY LI

"Harry, it's unanimous. We're formally inviting you to move your family to Little Rock and join the staff of Mosaic." Though eight years have passed, I (Harry) still remember the moment Mark invited me to join him at Mosaic. I was standing in the front yard of my four-acre property overlooking some of the most beautiful scenery Idaho has to offer. We had a wonderful home and were quite comfortable where we were at the time. So you can understand why I found Mark's next words to be incredibly challenging and frightening: "You need to understand that we don't have a lot of money, but we *think* we can pay you at least two thousand dollars a month from the offerings. Beyond that, you'll have to raise support or somehow bring the rest with you."

And that was it! No contract. No job description. No fringe benefits. Nothing but a simple phone call placed and received in naive faith. I remember telling Mark that my wife, Melanie, and I would need some time to talk things over, but somehow, deep inside, I knew what my answer would be. We had already sensed that the Lord was calling us to become part of this unique church, and when the offer came, it was clear to both of us what we had to do. We were more afraid of saying no to God than we were of saying yes to him, despite our apprehensions.

I had met Mark just six months earlier while on a business trip to Arkansas. I was only visiting Little Rock for a day, and looking back over the past years, I can now see that this was one of those God-ordained appointments! At that time in my life, I was teaching at a university, but I had been considering the possibility of leaving the academic world to serve in full-time ministry. Mark and I met at a local coffee shop, and for the next few hours he painted a picture for me: a vision of a diverse church — on earth as it is in heaven — the very church he was hoping Mosaic would become. I had never heard of a multi-ethnic church, nor had I ever entertained the thought of joining such a ministry. But the vision of Mosaic instantly captured my heart.

At the time, I was also in discussion with several other churches about possible ministry positions. These were well-established churches offering real salaries with real benefits! But there was just something about the vision of Mosaic that kept tugging at my heart. My wife and I would make two more trips to Little Rock before that fateful day on which I called Mark to accept the official "offer." Looking back on that time, I now laugh out loud. It felt like we were taking such a big step of faith leaving the security of the academic world and the personal comforts of our scenic home. But now I realize that it was just a tiny step compared with the leaps and bounds of faith that have been required of us to help establish this church over the past eight years.

Like the expedition of those pioneers in the United States who once headed west, pursuit of a healthy multi-ethnic church is a journey fraught with difficulty, uncertainty, and personal peril. Yet every ounce of energy expended, every tear I've shed, every cry of desperation has been so richly rewarded in seeing God's impressive glory displayed in the unity and diversity of our people. Indeed, what a privilege it's been to witness his merciful work in the lives of those who have chosen to journey with us in becoming part of something so much bigger than ourselves.

To realize the dream of a multi-ethnic church requires that church pastors, planters, and lay leaders know the certainty of their calling and demands steady faith, personal courage, and a willingness to sacrifice. Yet make no mistake: the success of a church like Mosaic is a testimony to the grace of God. More often than not, I believe, he works in spite of our failures and shortcomings as we faithfully respond to his vision for the church.

Like Mark, I believe that the unity of diverse believers walking, working, and worshiping God together as one is at the very heart and center of God's desire for the local church. And we are convinced that believers should and must come together as one in the local church despite personal preferences, challenges, and obstacles. As Jesus recognizes in John 17:20–23, such unity becomes a living demonstration to the world of the gospel's power to transform lives. This unity testifies to the power of the gospel to break through the dividing walls of ethnic segregation, hatred, and animosity that are still so evident in our world today. It is a daily witness to God's love for all people, a love displayed through our own genuine love for others different from ourselves. Indeed, in the multi-ethnic church, the power and pleasure of God resides in a most unique way!

Revelation 7:9–12 gives us an astounding vision of the future: men and women from every nation, tribe, people, and tongue will one day gather before the throne and worship God with one voice for all eternity. If this is the future of the church, can there be any doubt that God is pleased to see us pursuing such a vision here on earth? We often ask ourselves, "If the kingdom of heaven is not segregated, why on earth is the church?"

Our church is truly a mosaic of broken individuals, yet united together, we form one beautiful picture in Christ. I'm so thankful that God has blessed our work in ways no person could ever take credit for. Thankfully, his supernatural provisions and awesome displays of power remain as evident today as they were in the beginning, when I first arrived in Little Rock to help blaze a trail. Both Mark and I hope that after reading this book, you too will join us on this road less traveled. And we hope your own efforts, and contributions to the multi-ethnic church movement, will someday make the road even wider for the masses soon heading our way.

LET US POUR YOUR CUP

Now that we've provided some context and personal introductions, let me (Mark) outline the rest of the book.

For the convenience of those who have not read my book *Building a Healthy Multi-ethnic Church*, I will summarize the biblical mandate and core commitments of a multi-ethnic church in chapter 1. In chapters 2 through 8, we will address seven common challenges or obstacles that must be overcome by multi-ethnic church planters, pastors, and ministry leaders in pursuit of the vision. Following this, I will provide a brief conclusion.

Throughout these pages, we will also offer real-time insights and chronicle lessons learned through the story of Mosaic. In so doing, we'll take you beyond needs to the more practical challenges and ramifications of day-to-day leadership within a multi-ethnic church. In addition, each chapter (2–8) will provide the voice and insights of multi-ethnic church leaders from around the country, friends and fellow pioneers who are experienced and accomplished in the field. For further information and demographic data concerning their ministries, see appendix 1. And at the end of each chapter, you will find discussion questions for use by leadership teams, in small groups throughout the church, or simply to guide your own private reflection.

Oh, and by the way, whenever the first person is used throughout the book, you can assume it is me talking, unless otherwise indicated by use of Harry's name in parentheses. (Sometimes I'll indicate my own name, just to be clear.)

So grab a cup of coffee (if you like), and let's get going! There's a lot for us to talk about as we seek to establish local churches that reflect, in more than mere words, the love of God for all people on earth as it is in heaven, as we seek to brew ethnic blends!

QUESTIONS FOR REFLECTION AND DISCUSSION

1. When was the first time you recognized that local churches are largely segregated along ethnic and economic lines? Where or how old were you at the time? What, if anything, bothered you about what you observed? Why do you think you had such feelings?

2. Why did you purchase this book? What has shaped your interest in the multi-ethnic church at this time?

3. How diverse is the church you attend, serve, or lead? If 20 percent or more of the people attending your church on a Sunday morning are of different ethnic origin than that of the majority of people who attend, why do you think this is so? If not, what factors or barriers can you identify that may be keeping diverse others from getting involved?

4. Are you aware of a healthy multi-ethnic church in your area? What do you know about the church? Can you see yourself ever attending or serving as a pastor in such a church? What excites you about the possibilities; what fears or concerns might you have when you imagine yourself involved?

5. What key thought, revelation, or insight will you take away from this chapter? What is God asking you to do in response?

I'LL DRINK TO THAT!

Mandate and Commitments of a Diverse Congregation

May they be brought to complete unity to let the world know that you sent me and have loved them even as you have loved me.

— John 17:23

THE NEW NORMAL

At one time on my nightstand was David T. Olson's book *The American Church in Crisis* (Grand Rapids, Mich.: Zondervan, 2008). Olson is the director of the American Research Project and director of church planting for the Evangelical Covenant Church. Loaded with charts, graphs, and sidebars, Olson's book presents research and conclusions based on his study of a national database of some two hundred thousand churches.

And there is cause for concern.

For instance, despite some optimistic polls that suggest the American church is thriving, Olson writes, "On any given Sunday, the vast majority of Americans are absent from church and if trends continue, by 2050, the percentage of Americans attending church will be half [of what it was in 1990]." To avoid this dismal future, Olson suggests, "the American church must engage with ... three critical transitions ... which have altered the relationship between American culture and the church." He defines these as:

1. The transition from a Christian to a post-Christian society
2. The transition from a modern to a postmodern society
3. The transition from a mono-ethnic to a multi-ethnic society

Of course, the first two transitions have long been foreseen and understood. It's the third transition — "the new kid on the block" — that's getting increased attention from researchers, writers, theologians, and practitioners alike. Yes, growing numbers are now recognizing that the multi-ethnic church is not only a pragmatic response but also, and more important, a biblical response to address these changing times. According to Olson, it's not only what's needed; it's the future!

He writes, "In the mono-ethnic world, Christians, pastors and churches only had to understand their own culture. Ministering in a homogeneous culture is easier, but mono-ethnic Christianity can gradually become culture-bound.... In the multi-ethnic world, pastors, churches and Christians need to operate under the rules of the early church's mission to the Gentiles." And I really loved this statement: "As the power center of [global] Christianity moves south and east, the multi-ethnic church is becoming the normal and natural picture of the new face of Christianity."[1]

CHANGE HAS COME TO AMERICA

Beyond the research, the historic race for the presidency and election results of 2008 now overwhelmingly confirm that demographic shifts throughout the United States have brought change to America. With this in mind, local church planters and pastors can no longer afford to ignore consideration of the implications for their own ministries or the people they seek to influence in the future. Failure on our part to recognize the changing landscape or to adapt in accordance with Scripture may soon render our work, or worse yet our message, irrelevant. For in an increasingly diverse and cynical society, people will no longer find credible the message of God's love for all people when it's proclaimed from segregated churches. In these changing times, those without Christ will respond not to platitudes but rather to practice, not to words but only to an authentic witness of God's love for all people that is daily displayed in life and action. And I believe that this witness is best matured and manifested through healthy multiethnic churches.

The desire to establish multi-ethnic churches, however, must not be rooted in the fact that Tiger Woods is biracial and somehow representative of the changing face of America, or for that matter in Rodney King's emotional appeal, "People ... can we all get along?" Nor should we pursue the dream simply because the neighborhood is changing, because the increasing diversification of certain states has rendered them majority-minority, or because the latest projections indicate that the entire nation will be so declared by 2042.[2] This is all well and good, making conditions now favorable for our attempts. Rather, the pursuit of ethnic blends must be firmly rooted in God's Word.

In other words, it's not about racial reconciliation; it's about reconciling men and women to God through faith in Jesus Christ, and about reconciling a local church to the principles and practices of New Testament congregations of faith, such as existed at Antioch and Ephesus. Yes, these churches were multi-ethnic, in and through which believing Jews and Gentiles gathered as one to tangibly express the peace, hope, and love of Christ before a lost and dying world. In so doing, men and women of various backgrounds — beyond the distinctions of this world that so often and otherwise divide — came together to obey the Great Commandment, declare a great compassion, and fulfill the Great Commission. Their unity of mind, heart, and purpose resulted in a great expansion of the gospel and in accomplishing God's will on earth as it is in heaven. Indeed, they were one in Christ and in the local church so the world would know God's love and believe!

Likewise, it's the unity of diverse believers walking, working, and worshiping God together as one in and through the local church that will provide for us the most effective means for reaching the world with the gospel in the twenty-first century!

What, though, you may ask, is the basis for such passion and hope? And why am I (and increasing numbers like me) so sure that in reflecting the diversity of heaven, the local church will newly proclaim the Prince of Peace on earth in reformation and power, resulting in the salvation of significant numbers of seekers and skeptics alike to the glory of God? Is this a realistic goal or only the wishful thinking of mystics and mavericks among us? I believe it is not only a realistic goal but also the very prayer and will of our Lord and Savior, Jesus Christ, for the local church. This, then, should serve to inspire our faith, courage, and sacrificial abandonment to the cause.

We should also recognize that the multi-ethnic church, and on a broader scale, the multi-ethnic church movement, represents nothing new; rather, it is reformative in nature. It was first envisioned by Christ (John 17:20 – 23), then described by Luke (Acts 11:19 – 26; 13:1), and ultimately prescribed by the apostle Paul throughout his writings, most notably in his letter to the Ephesians. Therefore we embrace the vision not because it is politically correct but because it is spiritually correct, and while it is not necessarily an easy vision to pursue, it is a sound ecclesiology.

Beyond the theological underpinnings of the movement, it is also important to recognize that certain values are present within, and indicative of, healthy multi-ethnic churches. Early research by George Yancey, published in his book *One Body, One Spirit,* first identified these as "principles of successful multi-racial churches."[3] Subsequent interaction with practitioners through the Mosaix Global Network, however, led to the further examination of these principles and their refinement.[4] From this process emerged what can now be described as the Seven Core Commitments of a Multi-ethnic Church.

The biblical mandate and the core commitments of a multi-ethnic church are fully developed in my book *Building a Healthy Multi-ethnic Church*. Through the remainder of this chapter, I will provide a short overview of these concepts as a prelude to discussing seven common challenges to mixing diversity into your local church. Before I do, however, let me define my terms.

WHAT SHOULD WE SAY?

Have you noticed that in different places, people will sometimes use different terms to describe a similar thing? The same is true when it comes to describing what I call the multi-ethnic church. In my mind, it's not important that everyone, everywhere, use the same term in this regard. What is important, however, is that people speaking of the issue define their terms to avoid confusion.

I do not use the term *multicultural* to describe Mosaic or other such churches in order to avoid any confusion with the tenets of multiculturalism — otherwise defined as "postmodern universalism" or "the doctrine of tolerance" (which, by the way, is the antithesis of love) — all too prevalent on college campuses throughout the United States today. Furthermore, I do not describe our church as multiracial, because as a pastor and theologian, I believe the Bible makes it clear that there is only one race — the human race — comprised of many different ethnicities (*ethne*, Greek plural, as used in Acts 17:26, for example, where we are told God "made from one man every nation [*ethnos*, Greek singular] of mankind" [NASB]). Therefore I use the term *multi-ethnic* in an attempt to be more biblically precise. In addition, when I speak of a healthy multi-ethnic church, I mean to imply the economic, educational, and generational diversity that ought to be present as well. In fact, I often say that ethnic and economic diversity are two sides of the same coin and should be considered equally by church planters and pastors seeking to establish a church for all people.

THE BIBLICAL MANDATE OF THE MULTI-ETHNIC CHURCH

Of course, God's heart for the nations is made clear in the Bible, from the book of Genesis through the apostle John's writing in the book of Revelation. Sadly, however, the general narrative has not necessarily informed local church development through the years. In other words, while pastors may lead their congregants into foreign missions or to be involved with local outreach or community service, loving diverse others has largely remained something we do, more than a reflection of who we are for the sake of the gospel.

Yet make no mistake: the intentional planting and development of local churches that reflect God's love for all people — the unity and diversity of God's kingdom on earth as it is in heaven — is not optional in the New Testament; it is mandated. In fact, there are three key theological insights that support this claim.

Envisioned by Christ (John 17:20 – 23)

On the night before he died, Christ prayed specifically that future generations of believers would be united as one so that the world would know God's love and believe. In this way and by this means, Christ stated that his mission would be accomplished through others and, ultimately, that his Father would be glorified. What Jesus intends for us (the local church), then, is clear: we have been called to be one for the sake of the gospel. It may not be easy, but it is biblical, and it is right. Therefore we are to "walk in a manner worthy of the calling with which [we] have been called" (Eph. 4:1 NASB).

It is significant to realize that Christ prayed we would be one for two very specific reasons, or "so that" two things will occur. The words *so that* in verses 21 and 23 are translated from the Greek word *hina*. This word, a preposition, is used linguistically to introduce what Greek scholars refer to as a "hina clause." In the Koine Greek of the New Testament, a hina clause introduces an "if-then" propositional truth. In essence, the proposition can be stated as follows: if X occurs (though there's no guarantee that it will), then Y is the guaranteed result. With this in mind, we can paraphrase John 17:20 – 23 to read, "I also want to pray for those who, in time, will come to believe in me through the witness of my disciples.... Yes, I pray that those who come after them will be completely united as one. There is no guarantee that they will be one, but if they will, there are two guaranteed results. First, men and women throughout the world will recognize that I am the Messiah. In addition, men and women throughout the world will recognize that you, Father, love them. They will respond to your love and receive eternal life through faith in me."

When men and women of diverse backgrounds walk together as one in Christ in and through the local church, they reflect the Father's love for all people. More than that, a oneness of mind, love, spirit, and purpose proclaims the gospel in a most powerful, tangible, and compelling way. For as his own union with the Father uniquely empowered Christ to proclaim God's love for the world, our union with him and, he says, with fellow believers uniquely empowers us to do the same. Yes, in pursuing the "perfection of unity," we will see the world come to know him as we do!

Described by Luke (Acts 11:19 – 26; 13:1)

Have you ever noticed that it's not until Luke is nearly halfway through the book of Acts (Acts 11:18) that he can state with confidence that the leaders of the church in Jerusalem understand that the gospel, like the church, is not just for the Jews but for everyone — Jews and Gentiles alike? The next verse, though, makes it clear that the issue had not yet been settled for everyone. For those who were driven from Jerusalem following the stoning of Stephen "made their way to Phoenicia and Cyprus and Antioch, speaking the word to no one except to Jews" (Acts 11:19 NASB). This would be disheartening if not for what Luke reports next: "But there were some of them, men of Cyprus and Cyrene, who came to Antioch and began speaking to the Greeks also, preaching the Lord Jesus" (Acts 11:20 NASB). In other words, there were some who said, "I'm not going home; I'm going to Antioch, and I'm not just going to speak to my own people. I'm going to speak to anyone who will listen!" This was a truly significant step and, in my opinion, the most pivotal moment in the entire New Testament concerning the growth and development of the church, for the following reasons.

First, the evangelists and church planters mentioned in Acts 11:20 were men of diverse cultural backgrounds. Second, they intentionally went to Antioch to speak not only to the Jews but also to the Greeks (Gentiles). It should come as no surprise to learn that "the hand of the Lord was with them" (Acts 11:21 NASB). In fact, three times in Acts 11:21 – 26 we read the phrase "large number" or "considerable numbers," twice in connection with conversion and once in the context of discipleship.

So Jews loved Gentiles, Gentiles loved Jews, and they were all worshiping God together as one in the local church at Antioch. In addition, the church was the first to take up a collection for fellow believers living in a foreign land (Acts 11:28 – 30). Its pastoral leadership team included two men from Africa, one from the Mediterranean, one from Asia Minor, and one from the Middle East (Acts 4:36; 9:11; 13:1), providing the church a visible witness and a model of unity at the highest level. And it was the church at Antioch, and not the church in Jerusalem, that first sent missionaries to the world. With these things in mind, it's not coincidental that the disciples were first called Christians at Antioch (Acts 11:26). For there Christ was clearly recognized in the midst of unity, just as he had said he would be (John 17:23).

It is the multi-ethnic church at Antioch, then, and not the homogeneous church at Jerusalem, that should serve as our primary model for local church development in the twenty-first century. Yes, it is the church at Antioch, and not the church in Jerusalem, that is the most influential church of the entire New Testament.

Prescribed by Paul (Ephesians)

Biblical evidence does not support the notion of a homogeneous church at Ephesus. The fact is, the local church at Ephesus was made up of both Jewish and Gentile converts and thus was multi-ethnic (Acts 19:8 – 17; 20:21). With this in mind, the theme of Paul's letter to the Ephesians can be stated as follows: the unity of the church for the sake of the gospel.

Following his comments concerning an individual believer's unity with the Father through faith in Jesus Christ (chapter 1) and concerning the unity of Jews and Gentiles — the two groups now "one new man and body" — (chapter 2), Paul intends next to share with the Ephesians his prayers for them (Eph. 3:1, 14 – 19). However, he momentarily interrupts himself to remind the congregation of his apostolic mission. In Ephesians 3:2 – 13, a parenthetical statement is inserted in which he defines his calling and declares that "by revelation there was made known to me the mystery ... of Christ" (Eph. 3:3 – 4 NASB). Here too he mentions a previous letter he had written to the church, in which he had also addressed his "insight into the mystery of Christ" (Eph. 3:4 NASB). According to Paul, understanding of this mystery had not been granted to past generations but had only "now been revealed by the Spirit to God's holy apostles and prophets" (Eph. 3:5).

A common error is to assume that the mystery Paul is speaking of is, simply, the mystery of the gospel — the good-news message of Christ's life, death, and resurrection, his atonement for sin. Yet this is not the case. For in verse 6, Paul makes it clear that the mystery of Christ is something altogether different: "To be specific, that the Gentiles are fellow heirs and fellow members of the body, and fellow partakers of the promise in Christ Jesus through the gospel" (Eph. 3:6 NASB). The New International Version translates the verse this way: "This mystery is that through the gospel the Gentiles are heirs together with Israel, members together of one body, and sharers together in the promise in Christ Jesus."

I believe that this verse represents the very apex of the book, from which all else written derives its context and meaning. In fact, it represents the very substance of Paul's life and ministry. Here, Paul is describing himself not merely as a minister of the gospel but also a minister of the mystery of Christ. Notice too that he calls himself a minister of "this" gospel (Eph. 3:7), that is, of the good news concerning the unity of Jews and Gentiles in the church. Such understanding is further supported by his words near the end of the letter, at which time he asks the Ephesians to "pray also for me ... so that I will fearlessly make known the mystery of the gospel, *for which I am an ambassador in chains*" (Eph. 6:19 – 20, emphasis mine). As Paul writes this letter from prison, then, he is in chains not simply for proclaiming the gospel but also for proclaiming the mystery of Christ (Col. 4:2 – 4), the mystery of the gospel, namely, "that the Gentiles are fellow heirs [together with the Jews] ... and fellow partakers of the promise in Christ Jesus through the gospel" (Eph. 3:6 NASB).

SEVEN CORE COMMITMENTS OF A MULTI-ETHNIC CHURCH

Clearly, then, the Scriptures emphasize the importance and necessity of the multi-ethnic church as a witness to the credibility of the gospel message. To build a healthy muti-ethnic church today, however, there are seven core commitments that church planters, pastors, and ministry leaders will need to adopt and apply.

1. Embrace Dependence

In Matthew 17:14 – 21, Jesus heals a young boy of demonic seizures. When his disciples ask him, "Why couldn't we drive [the demon] out?" he replies, "Because you have so little faith.... This kind does not go out but by prayer and fasting." Likewise, the multi-ethnic church is a different kind of church. In other words, there are no simple solutions, no shortcuts or strategies of humankind that can accomplish what only God can do in this regard. In other words, it is a work of the Holy Spirit and of faith that cannot otherwise be attained through human means or efforts. Such a church can be established only when we commit ourselves to prayer, patience, and persistence in seeking to "walk [together as one with diverse others] in a manner worthy of the calling with which you [all] have been called" (Eph. 4:1 NASB).

2. Take Intentional Steps

While it is true that the multi-ethnic church is a work of God, it does not just happen. You must take intentional steps to turn the vision into reality. With this in mind, you should view a commitment to dependence and a commitment to intentionality as two sides of the same coin. For while it is true that the Vine (Christ) alone produces the fruit, it is the task of the branches (us) to bear it (John 15:4 – 8), and this you will do when you abide in him. Concerning the church, this means that pastors and planters must intentionally align the church with Christ's will and resist the urge to align it with their own.

Intentionality, then, is both an attitude and an action. It must permeate and inform every corridor of a multi-ethnic church. For instance, I have no doubt that people mean well when they say they would gladly welcome people of various ethnic or economic backgrounds to come be a part of "their" church. However, in practice, what they really mean is, "as long as they like things the way we do them." Therefore you should recognize that a healthy multi-ethnic church will be established not by assimilation but rather by accommodation.

Notice the subtle difference in terminology. The word *assimilate* means "to integrate somebody into a larger group so that differences are minimized or eliminated."[5] Yet the word *accommodate* means "to adjust actions in response to somebody's needs."[6] In other words, you must not ask or expect diverse others to check their culture at the door to become part of "your" church. Rather, it is the responsibility of those in the majority to adjust themselves intentionally, their own attitudes and actions, in order to enfold diverse others into the life of the growing, developing body.

In addition, to build a healthy multi-ethnic church, we must no longer allow the homogeneous unit principle to inform our understanding of success in church planting, growth, and development in the twenty-first century. I'll have more to say about this later in the book.

3. Empower Diverse Leaders

To build a healthy multi-ethnic church, you must also empower diverse leaders, from the pulpit to the nursery and at every stop in between, vocational and volunteer leaders alike. Credibility and modeling begins here, as Luke recognizes in Acts 13:1, where he lists the prophets and teachers at Antioch not only by name but also by country of origin (see also Acts 4:36; 9:11). However, it's important to recognize that when it comes to staffing for diversity, intentionality is the middle ground between quota and wishful thinking. In other words, you should not force the issue by predetermining just who or how many different kinds of people you will involve as leaders at a given time. On the other hand, you cannot simply sit in your office all day and pray that somehow a well-qualified candidate of diverse ethnic origin will simply appear at your door!

So let me ask you a question: Have you ever wondered why "the best person for the job" always looks like you? The reason, of course, is simple. When a position becomes available in most churches, leaders tend to contact those they know and trust, to inquire who they in turn might recommend for the job. The people we contact and those they recommend are, more often than not, people just like us in ethnic, economic, and educational background. Consequently, the people we know recommend people they know, and by the time decisions are made, the new hire — "the best person for the job" — looks just like us as well.

Therefore, those intent on building a healthy multi-ethnic church should develop relationships with people outside their own ethnic and economic background for just such a purpose. If starting from scratch, you can do this simply by picking up the phone and introducing yourself to diverse pastors and professors, ministry and business professionals alike, or by using a variety of other methods to make yourself and your desires known. If you couple this with passion, persistence, and prayer, you can expect your effort to be rewarded.

4. Develop Cross-cultural Relationships

Of course, personal relationships are important to the health and well-being of any church. In a multi-ethnic church, however, they are of exponentially greater importance! Indeed, relationships form the very foundation and fabric of a multi-ethnic church because trust is not a commodity so easily assumed in an environment where people must interact with others different from themselves. Cross-cultural relationships take time to form and cannot be agenda driven.

We should recognize that all of us from time to time have prejudicial thoughts and feelings because of past conditioning from family, social setting, peer interactions, community mores, and the media. The question is, What should be done with these thoughts and feelings when they arise?

The word *prejudice* can be defined as "a preformed opinion concerning someone or something." More often than not, the term is used to describe the negative or inaccurate opinions we have preformed of others with whom we have had (in most cases) little to no relational contact. It is true, however, that some people have had negative encounters with others different from themselves and that these experiences have, quite naturally, shaped their thoughts and feelings. Therefore, in attempting to encourage the development of cross-cultural relationships within the local church, we should be careful not to denigrate those who share honestly about themselves in this regard. Rather, to build a healthy multi-ethnic church, we should provide opportunities for open dialogue and commend those with both the courage to discuss such things and the determination to deal with them. When misunderstandings arise, we must determine (as in a marriage) to keep the ring on.

5. Pursue Cross-cultural Competence

The understanding we need in order to be effective in a cross-cultural environment is gained through experience and interaction with diverse people, especially those with whom we are one in the Lord. In this context, competence speaks of proficiency in addressing another's culture or customs, their needs and expectations different from our own. To build a healthy multi-ethnic church, we must commit ourselves to the pursuit of cross-cultural competence, whether that means becoming proficient in the idiosyncrasies of language or learning the ins and outs of traditions different from our own. Once acquired, cross-cultural competence allows us to interact in a more informed and effective way with others of various ethnic or economic backgrounds. In many ways, cross-cultural competence is more caught than taught.

Although competence does not assume expertise, it does describe a general aptitude in working with people of various cultures. More specifically, it defines individuals who "value diversity, conduct self-assessment, manage the dynamics of difference, acquire and institutionalize cultural knowledge and are able to adapt to diversity and the cultural contexts of the communities they serve."[7] Pastoral leaders can no longer afford to be cross-culturally incompetent in an increasingly interconnected world. In pursuit of cross-cultural competence, those seeking to establish a multi-ethnic church should surround themselves with cross-culturally competent people who can be trusted to provide insight and training across the board, from the nursery to the pulpit and at every station in between. In so doing, you will expedite the process and avoid many unnecessary mistakes along the way.

Pursuit of cross-cultural competence moves us beyond ourselves toward a deeper understanding of life from another's perspective. Such reflections should draw us nearer to others who are not like us and, together with them, nearer to Christ in and through the local church.

6. Promote a Spirit of Inclusion

Two thousand years ago Paul commanded the church at Philippi to "do nothing from selfishness or empty conceit, but with humility of mind regard one another as more important than yourselves; do not merely look out for your own personal interests, but also for the interests of others" (Phil. 2:3 – 4 NASB). In other words, Paul expects individuals in a congregation not to look inward but to get beyond themselves for the benefit of others. His words should inspire our present-day attitude toward and approach to creating an environment in which diverse people not only feel welcome but also, in time, feel they are a significant part of the whole. Believers who embrace this imperative will find that they are able to worship God joyfully even at times, for example, when the music played on a Sunday morning is not compatible with their own personal tastes, when someone prays a prayer in a language they do not understand, or when in some other way things are not done in accordance with their preferences.

To promote a spirit of inclusion, you must also pay attention to those little things that add up to create the look and feel of the whole. At Mosaic, for example, all of our signage is produced both in English and Spanish, as are the bulletins and PowerPoint slides. And we fly flags in our church to represent the diversity of nations within our body. Such considerations, though seemingly inconsequential, demonstrate to others a great deal about who we are and what we value.

A commitment to promote a spirit of inclusion, however, in no way implies a commitment to embrace doctrines or practices that in one way or another violate the Word of God. On the other hand, promoting a spirit of inclusion will require us to be patient with genuine seekers — those new to the faith and those disenfranchised who are reconnecting with Christ and his church after a season of sin, hurt, or absence. Ultimately, the goal is to create an environment where all people feel welcome, where truth is proclaimed, where grace and mercy abound.

7. Mobilize for Impact

The intended outcome of establishing a multi-ethnic church is not unity for unity's sake. Rather, it is to turn the power and pleasure of God — uniquely expressed in a church where diverse people "are being built together to become a dwelling in which God lives by his Spirit" (Eph. 2:22) — outward in order to bless the city, lead people to Christ, encourage the greater body, and fulfill the Great Commission (Matt. 28:19–20).

Yes, in the future we must speak with one voice, one heart, and one message to win the world for Jesus. And through multi-ethnic churches, we can do just that as we diligently proclaim and "preserve the unity of the Spirit in the bond of peace. [For] there is one body and one Spirit, just as also you were called in one hope of your calling; one Lord, one faith, one baptism, one God and Father of all who is over all and through all and in all" (Eph. 4:3–6 NASB).

Having summarized the biblical mandate for the multi-ethnic church and shared the seven core commitments that are required to make it a reality, we will now turn our attention to seven common challenges you will likely face in pursuit of ethnic blends. But before we do, consider the following profound words of Chris Rice from his book *More Than Equals*: "Yes, deep reconciliation will produce justice, and new relationships between the races. This will lead Christians to become a bright light in the public square. But I have become convinced that God is not very interested in the church healing the race problem. I believe it is more true that God is using race to heal the church."[8]

QUESTIONS FOR REFLECTION AND DISCUSSION

1. Review and discuss David Olson's insights concerning the three critical transitions facing the church in the twenty-first century (see p. 36). What is your understanding of each? How do you see such things affecting your church at this moment?

2. What are the two primary reasons why the authors believe pastors and church planters should seek to establish multi-ethnic congregations today (see pp. 40 – 41)? What other factors should or should not drive our motivations?

3. In your own words, can you articulate the biblical mandate for the multi-ethnic church? What insights stood out to you in reading or reflecting on the three New Testament passages that make the case as discussed in this chapter? Are there other critical passages to consider? Explain your answer.

4. In your own words, can you articulate the seven core commitments of a multi-ethnic church? What insights stood out to you in reading or reflecting on the commitments as discussed in this chapter? Are there other critical principles to consider? Explain your answer.

5. What key thought, revelation, or insight will you take away from this chapter? What is God asking you to do in response?

Chapter 2

BLENDING AS A FAMILY

Overcoming the Personal Obstacles

Let us not become weary in doing good, for at the proper
time we will reap a harvest if we do not give up.
— *Galatians 6:9*

ONE THING LEADS TO ANOTHER

On May 17, 2001, after nearly eighteen months of consideration,
exploration, and prayer concerning the future, my wife, Linda,
and I received a phone call that would determine the next season
of our ministry. It was a call that would change our lives forever.

For eighteen years I had served as a pastor to students in
churches throughout Arizona, Oregon, Washington, and
Arkansas. Linda and I had even spent two years working with
American military dependents stationed at Ramstein Air Force
Base in Germany. Now, though, after I had weighed my options
and was certain that it was time to embrace the responsibilities
of senior pastoral leadership, two possibilities remained on the
table. Either I would join the staff of Scottsdale Bible Church
in Scottsdale, Arizona, or I would stay in Little Rock to plant
a multi-ethnic and economically diverse church in the heart of
central Arkansas — a church founded in response to the prayer
of Jesus Christ for unity (John 17:20 – 23) and patterned after
the New Testament church at Antioch (Acts 11:19 – 26; 13:1), a
church we would call Mosaic.

Scottsdale Bible was well established and represented a very logical, next-step progression in my ministry career. For nearly twenty-five years it had grown under the leadership of Dr. Darryl DelHousaye, widely recognized as a strong teacher of the Word with a genuine heart for people.[1] And it had everything a young man in transition could want: thousands of people, strong programs for children and youth, a large campus, a great reputation, a vision for continued expansion, and, best of all, a well-funded salary! I would become the directional leader of a growing congregation (venue) within the church, consisting of more than fifteen hundred people meeting on Sunday evenings in two services. In addition, the church was attractively located in my own hometown, where my aging mother was still living alone. In many ways, I was certain that God was leading me to serve this healthy but otherwise homogeneous church.

On the other hand, Mosaic was nothing more than a dream — a strongly compelling one, however, given all that I was beginning to understand about the multi-ethnic nature of the New Testament church. Would taking the job in Scottsdale somehow compromise my newfound insights? Should I accept the position simply because it was so clearly the easier, more logical thing to do? Could I someday live with myself when leaned back, feet propped up, and a cold one in hand, I might wonder, "What if I would have stayed in Little Rock to plant Mosaic?"

To know for sure, Linda and I decided to place a fleece before God in prayer. If Scottsdale Bible Church offered me the job, I would take it in faith, believing it was his will. If the church did not, I would know beyond any shadow of doubt that I was to pursue the vision of Mosaic. In other words, we decided to place our future entirely into his hands.

In May 2001 I flew to Arizona for a final meeting with the leadership of Scottsdale Bible. In many ways, it was more a formality, as I had been in discussion with the church for quite some time. In fact, just a few months prior the church had flown the Sunday evening worship pastor and his wife to Little Rock in order for us to get to know one another as couples. At the time I was told, "If you all get along, then it's a done deal; that's how we'll know God's in this." Well, the four of us did hit it off, and following the visit, I had no reason to doubt I would be hired. I even had friends on staff at the church, many of whom I had known for years, all putting in good words for me and by this time providing me with a very positive inside scoop; in their opinion, it was just a matter of time.

So here I was in what was to be a final interview with Darryl, a few others from his executive team, and three elders representing the board. I had only to clear this hurdle, and the job was mine! But somewhere during our time together, I felt a question stir inside. It was a systemic question, fundamental to my understanding of the position and consequently to my future. Yet I hesitated to ask it, somehow aware that in raising the issue I could jeopardize the opportunity altogether. All I had to do was keep my mouth shut, and I would soon be moving home to Arizona! But the longer I sat there, the more I felt compelled to speak up. It would be the only way I could be certain of God's will.

Taking a deep breath then, just before the meeting concluded, I found the courage to ask, "Are you looking for a leader or a manager to serve in this position?"

And for a moment the room fell silent, truly deer-in-the-headlights still.

Now, I don't recall exactly what was said in response, but I do remember that a somewhat mumbled, uncertain discussion began among those present. Soon after, the meeting adjourned without ever yielding a clear answer to my question, let alone the official "Welcome to the team!" I had expected to hear. Somewhat confused, I flew home to Arkansas the next day wondering, "Oh, Lord, what have I done?"

Three days later on a Thursday afternoon, Darryl finally called to follow up the visit. "Mark," he said, "that was a great question you asked the other day, and honestly, we had not yet considered it ourselves. Having since done so, we now believe this church is not ready to bring on a second leader, and a leader is clearly who you are. What we're really looking for in this next hire is a manager, and to a man we all agree: you are well positioned to remain in Little Rock and to plant Mosaic. In fact, we think you should do so!"

I received the call at home that day; Linda too was there. And after sharing Darryl's words with her, there was nothing left to say. God clearly had spoken, and we realized there was now a choice to make. We could second-guess ourselves, rationalizing the fleece as mere gimmick, and run from God, as Jonah did, or we could immediately heed the call, as did Abram when the Lord so clearly spoke to him some four thousand years ago, saying, "Leave your country, your people and your father's household and go to the land I will show you" (Gen. 12:1). Fortunately, I have a strong wife, a true woman of faith, and together we were determined to obey.

So right then, hand in hand, we walked into our back yard and sat under a tree to prayerfully commit ourselves to planting a diverse congregation of faith in a city infamously associated with the American civil rights movement.[2] It was a truly significant moment, one in which we essentially cut the cord with all that was familiar to us — namely, the homogeneous church environment in which we had grown in Christ, trained for ministry, established relationships, and served quite comfortably for nearly twenty years. Later that evening at dinner, we made it official by announcing to our four children, "Guys, we're going to start a church!"

NOT FOR THE FAINT OF HEART

I share this story because it illustrates the innocent faith, emotional courage, and willingness to sacrifice that will be required of you to hear and heed the call to plant, pastor, or otherwise get involved with a multi-ethnic church. Make no mistake: pursuit of ethnic blends in your congregation is no easy task. It will stretch you and your family in ways that you cannot imagine.

Having tasted its refreshing flavor, however, I do not think I could ever again be satisfied to consistently drink from a homogeneous well.

The fact is, I'm convinced that the multi-ethnic church is God's will for pastors intent on establishing churches that reflect his heart for all people. Such churches will be based upon the principles and practices of congregations that existed at Antioch or Ephesus, at the very beginning of Christian community. In those days, the church was truly multi-ethnic: Jewish and Gentile converts learned to walk, work, and worship God together as one so that the world would know God's love and believe (John 17:23). Similarly in our day, I believe, there is little hope of seeing exponential kingdom expansion apart from the establishment of churches like these. For I believe that the message of God's love for all people will be viewed with increasing suspicion and disdain in this century if it is not tangibly expressed across demographic lines even through the local church.

As I recall, neither Linda nor I had any idea how naive our enthusiasm was in those early days, in planting Mosaic. Nor did we understand the personal challenges our entire family would face in the years ahead. That's probably a good thing! Perhaps we might not have found the strength to follow God faithfully into the unknown of multi-ethnic ministry. Now, though, having faced and overcome many of those challenges, I want to encourage you in the words of Paul: "The one who calls you is faithful and he will do it" (1 Thess. 5:24).

MISUNDERSTANDINGS

One of the first personal challenges you will inevitably face is misunderstanding. Yes, if you are interested in planting a multi-ethnic church, get used to being misunderstood, by both friends and colleagues. When you cast the vision, you will no doubt find that there are some who just don't get it — and others who don't *want* to get it! Many people will give you good reasons not to do it, all (seemingly) with your best interests in mind. In any case, you can expect frequent moments of discouragement that will test your faith and resolve. Allow God to use these times to strengthen and refine your determination. Remember that no vision worth pursuing is easily accomplished.

Like anyone discovering new truth or gaining fresh insight, you will naturally want to share with others the things you are learning and developing within the context of a multi-ethnic church. However, I encourage you to not push too hard, becoming dogmatic in your views or harsh in your criticisms of other existing churches or models. Rather, be patient with those who are slow to embrace the vision or who, in fact, walk away after only sampling your product.

In addition, realize that your goal is not to convince those who are resistant to the message but rather to create a new reality: a healthy multi-ethnic church for those who readily embrace the vision. Your primary focus is not to win arguments but to faithfully develop and lead such a church. For as Christ instructed his disciples, "No one sews a patch of unshrunk cloth on an old garment, for the patch will pull away from the garment, making the tear worse. Neither do men pour new wine into old wineskins. If they do, the skins will burst, the wine will run out and the wineskins will be ruined. No, they pour new wine into new wineskins, and both are preserved" (Matt. 9:16 – 17). In other words, leave those content with the old wine alone and focus your energy on the future: in due time both you and your efforts will be affirmed. And don't be surprised to find that the masses are not flocking your way overnight! We are still in the Pioneer Stage of this movement, and, sadly, the concept of a multi-ethnic church remains foreign to many people still today, even to leaders in the North American church.

Not long ago, at a national conference on church planting, an informal gathering was held for a small group of VIPs (Very Important Pastors) to provide them an opportunity for interaction with one of the plenary speakers — a nationally recognized pastor and the author of many books. Toward the end of the meeting, an African American pastor, the leader of a respected multi-ethnic church, entered the room. In spite of the fact that he was somewhat late, and not to mention the only person of color in the room, the meeting's host greeted him warmly, even inviting him to ask the final question. As this pastor would later recall, "There wasn't much time to think, and I hesitated for a moment to ask what was otherwise on my heart. But I went ahead anyway and asked, 'What do you think about the multi-ethnic church?' Without hesitation the speaker bluntly responded, 'I don't recommend it; it's just too difficult. People want to go to church with others who are like them, and I don't think there's anything wrong with that.'" Responses like these are not only insensitive; they can be personally discouraging to leaders pursuing the vision of the multi-ethnic church.

The fact is, the difficulty of a task is not a reason for us to avoid it. Aren't you glad that Jesus did not approach kingdom building with the same kind of attitude? For instance, can you imagine him refusing to leave the comforts of heaven for the distresses of earth, saying, "No way, Father; the cross is just too difficult to bear"? Or can you imagine the apostle Paul refusing to go to the Gentiles because believing Jews would rather worship with their own kind and saying, "I see nothing wrong with that"? Nowhere in Scripture are we given a pass not to pursue the will of God based on degree of difficulty. Rather the job of local church leadership is to align the church with the will of God in spite of what is in line with our own will or the conventional wisdom of people. In other words, it's about living in the supernatural, beyond our own abilities, and allowing the glory of God to be displayed in and through the local church, reflecting the one "who is able to do immeasurably more than all we ask or imagine, according to his power that … work[s] within us" (Eph. 3:20).[3]

Unfortunately, the speaker's comments that day are not unique. I believe they echo a self-focused, "what's in it for me" mentality that drives many of us in choosing the kind of church to attend, plant, or develop. But even more, this attitude reflects a significant lack of understanding regarding the vision, mission, and developmental strategy of the New Testament local church as envisioned by Christ, described by Luke, and prescribed by Paul.[4]

PUSHBACK AND REJECTION

Given the pervasive influence of the homogeneous unit principle, it is natural to expect a fair amount of pushback or even outright rejection of the multi-ethnic message, regardless of your presentation. Discouragement comes with the territory, and it will certainly tempt you at points to compromise your vision in favor of all that more naturally fits the desires of people. To fulfill the dream, you must remain firm in your conviction, faithful to the task, and focused.

How can you overcome personal feelings of discouragement? You must press on in spite of them! You must be determined to stay the course and to endure them all, confident that the Lord will rescue you, just as he did Paul. For as the great apostle himself encouraged, "Let us not become weary in doing good, for at the proper time we will reap a harvest if we do not give up" (Gal. 6:9). With such determination, you too can expect God to establish the vision through your efforts and, ultimately, to realize ethnic blends.

HOME IS WHERE THE HEART IS

Another very personal issue that Linda and I initially faced was the location of our home. In pursuing the multi-ethnic vision, we wondered if we would be required to move from the suburbs to the city. We had built our house just four years earlier, and we lived in a section of town generally considered (though it wasn't necessarily) white and affluent. Would its location now become a stumbling block to the very diverse population we were seeking to reach? Might we be seen in the future as somehow disingenuous or hypocritical for failing to leave the comforts of our own community for the discomforts of the city? Is relocation a prerequisite to building a healthy multi-ethnic church?

To resolve this issue, I sought the counsel of a well-respected African American pastor in Little Rock prior to launching the church. His words at that time were both enlightening and freeing. As best I remember, he said, "Mark, the issue is not where you live — whether in the city or the suburbs, whether in a nice home and neighborhood or in the city's center. Ultimately, people will judge your heart. If you are all about yourself, they will know it. If you have a heart for others, however, it will be clearly demonstrated through acts of kindness, mercy, justice, and compassion that make a difference in their lives and in the community. When you lead so as not to forget the needs of others or leave them behind, it will not matter where you live. When you seek the good of the people, the people will want what's good for you and your family as well."

Given the overwhelming task of planting a multi-ethnic church in Little Rock, we decided that relocation was not in the best interest of our family at the time. And true to the insights of this pastor, the growth and development of our church was largely unaffected by the location of our home.

Still, there are a number of well-meaning believers, community activists, and Christ-centered church leaders who have chosen to embrace urban life and ministry, living *with* the community. Some have done so with a desire to reconcile injustice, and others to reconcile their own feelings of guilt due to privilege. Some seek to bring change to the community, others to be changed through the experience. Some go to teach, others to learn; some to transform the inner city, others to be transformed within their own hearts. No matter the motive, I have discovered that there is no right or wrong answer to the question of relocation. Indeed, there are often a variety of factors that must be considered, and each situation is different. Be careful to weigh the matter prayerfully and not let the zeal of your passion lead you to neglect a sober consideration of the cost (Luke 14:28 – 30). Whatever you decide, try to make the decision that is best for you and your family, free of any internal (false) guilt or externally imposed expectations.

PERSONAL DEPENDENCE

As I (Harry) reflect upon my own journey, the personal challenges I have faced as a member and a leader of a multi-ethnic church are in one way or another related to my commitment to embrace dependence. I found that the transition from the stoic halls of the academy to a multi-ethnic church in Little Rock required an exercise of mental, emotional, and physical faith that I had not previously been challenged to perform.

Why is a willingness to embrace dependence such an essential ingredient to the pursuit of ethnic blends? I believe that the multi-ethnic church is a work of God and of the Holy Spirit that cannot otherwise be achieved through human means or efforts. If the dream were easily achieved, many more diverse congregations would exist today. Yes, the unique challenges of multi-ethnic ministry are unlike anything you are likely to have faced in attending or serving a healthy homogeneous church. And because so few to date have realized the dream, you can't easily find the answers you need, nor is there an abundance of mentors ready to coach you through various issues you will encounter for the first time. Hopefully, that will change. In the meantime you'll need to engage your calling with eyes wide open and prepare yourself emotionally for the personal challenges of faith, courage, and sacrifice that lie ahead.

DOLLARS AND SENSE

Perhaps the greatest challenge I faced in coming to the church was in trusting God for my financial provision. In many cases, those attending ethnically diverse congregations are economically diverse as well. Consequently, I suspect, you too will be challenged at points to trust God to come through for you financially, in meeting your personal needs and the needs of the church you are seeking to lead.

For example, when Mark invited me to join the staff at Mosaic, he said the church could offer me only a small monthly salary. Whatever our family would need above and beyond that would have to be raised by way of support or somehow realized through other means. Mosaic simply did not have the financial horsepower to aggressively hire new people, and in those days, those who were on staff were required to raise most if not all of their salaries just for the privilege of working there! While I was excited about the opportunities for ministry, raising funds was not something I was all that excited to do.

It wasn't until I had accepted the offer from the church that I started doing the math. And that's when reality began to set in. I realized that there was a significant difference between what I was making as a tenured professor of engineering in a major university and the annual salary being offered by a one-hundred-and-fifty-member church plant. At the time, I figured that, having quit my job and moved my family to Little Rock, it would take us ten years to recover financially! For me, the cost I was admonished to consider (Luke 14:28) quickly morphed from an abstract spiritual concept into a very real, exact number—one with a lot of zeros on the end!

Amazingly, when we stepped forward in obedience to God's call, we found that he wonderfully provided for us after we arrived in Little Rock, far beyond the salary I was initially promised and in ways I had never dreamed possible. The university graciously allowed me a one-year transition period so that I could smoothly hand off all my research projects to a colleague. This enabled my family and me to move immediately to Little Rock instead of spending the months or even years typically required to raise that much financial support. For twelve months I continued to work for the university remotely at one-half of my former salary, and this made up the difference that we needed to make it through our first year at Mosaic.

And that was just the beginning of our experience with God's generous provision. The wonderful house that we owned in Idaho was sold without ever being listed on the market, the profit supplying us with what we would have needed to raise in support for our second year in Little Rock. Whenever there was a financial need, God provided in one way or another, many times as a direct result of prayers spoken to no one other than the Lord. Time after time, everything — from funds for our initial moving expenses to coverage of our health insurance premiums, and more — was supplied to us through amazing displays of God's goodness in response to faith and obedience.

At the beginning of my third year, the elders decided to begin transitioning the staff from outside support to internal salaries covered in full through the offerings. By God's grace, the church had grown numerically, and so had our offerings. The timing was right, and this decision reflected a sincere desire of leadership to mature the organization.

Ministering at Mosaic has not led my family and me to acquire great wealth, but we have been blessed beyond our wildest imagination, and every need has been met. We have experienced the fulfillment of many promises of Scripture and have seen that God will provide whatever is necessary for those who follow his calling, and that he will straighten the paths of those who trust him with all their heart. As you embrace dependence and walk not by might or power, or by human means or efforts, I believe God will not only provide for you too but also, more important, endow you with deeper faith — apart from which you cannot please him (Heb. 11:6).

CONSIDER THE COST

In addition, you will likely be called upon to give up most if not all of what is familiar or otherwise comfortable in pursuit of ethnic blends. In my case, I had spent ten years in academia building a research program, and many good things were happening. I had a stable of graduate research assistants at my disposal, was working with colleagues from around the country on cutting-edge projects, and was the coauthor of a bestselling textbook on integrated

HOLY DISCONTENT

Wayne Schmidt, Founding Pastor
Kentwood Community Church, Kentwood, Michigan

In August of 2005 I sat in the Leadership Summit as Bill Hybels challenged us to identify our "holy discontent." In that moment, God broke through with a penetrating question: "Wayne, is Kentwood Community Church (KCC) called to permeate the *whole* community with the good news of Jesus Christ, or just those in the community who look like you?"

When we launched KCC in 1979, the community around us was 97 percent white. Our church remained that way while our community changed to around 30 percent ethnic minority. Students in our local public schools now have birth certificates originating in fifty different nations. We no longer reflected our community—or heaven (Rev. 7:9).

Because I grew up in a setting with essentially no ethnic diversity, I was slow to perceive how God was calling us as a church to change. When that holy discontent was birthed within me, I felt I needed to spend a couple of years learning before I started leading KCC through this transition. However, God had been trying to get through to me repeatedly over the years, and too much time had been lost to spend extended time only learning. The challenge? I had to learn and lead simultaneously.

I read everything I could get my hands on. I participated in church-based seminars and community-based experiences such as the Institute for Healing Racism. Most of all, I approached people of color I trusted and asked them to be the "safe people for me to ask my dumb questions." They sensed my sincerity and I experienced their grace.

The holy discontent I carried resonated with our whole staff, our board of elders, and most of our congregation. We officially adopted a goal to have no more than 80 percent of one ethnicity in our weekend services by the year 2020, with the ultimate aim of reflecting the ethnic makeup of our community. We intentionally pursued a pathway to diversity based on the seven principles of effective multiracial churches outlined in Dr. George Yancey's book *One Body, One Spirit*. By God's grace, we are approaching our goal years ahead of schedule!

We started small, but we were committed not to "[despise] the day of small things" (Zech. 4:10). We believed that being faithful in little things would prepare us to be trusted with more (Luke 16:10). As we took baby steps, God began to draw people and resources to our church to fuel our journey forward.

It is true that learning and leading simultaneously leads to some rookie mistakes that at times hurt people or hinder your progress. But I've also been blessed to experience and to learn some wonderful realities along
cont.

the way. For instance, I have learned the following:

1. People you lead love to learn with you, to join you in the journey. Your mistakes, when readily admitted, keep them from being paralyzed by attempted perfectionism. You're not an expert instructing them but a fellow journeyer discovering along with them.

2. When people sense sincerity in your heart, it prompts a "love [that] covers a multitude of sins" (1 Peter 4:8 NASB). I have been amazed at how forgiving people have been of my leadership lapses when they see progress brought about through humility and intentionality.

3. When you have so much to learn, it causes you to listen more, and one of the greatest gifts we can give to those we lead is to be a good listener.

As the progress brought about by obedience overwhelms the paralysis arising from ignorance, we're seeing a church (KCC) that is "mak[ing] disciples of all [ethnicities]" (Matt. 28:19) come to life!

circuit design. There was absolutely nothing about my current job or situation that I didn't like! So as the vision for multi-ethnic ministry grew within my heart, I had to ask some tough personal questions: Am I willing to turn my back on a profession I have spent years developing to do something for which I have absolutely no formal training and only minimal part-time experience? Do I have the courage to follow God's lead? Will I get burned? Am I a fool?

During this period of consideration, I would often awake in a panic, thinking of all that could go wrong in moving to Little Rock. It was as if a daily debate was being waged in my spirit: Should I go or stay, remain a professor or become a pastor, enjoy the measure of status and notoriety I had gained in my field or step away from it all, down into the relative obscurity of church planting in a desperately needy area of the city? There was so much to consider, so much at stake, so many questions that day after day remained unanswered.

To gain clarity, I began to practice a discipline of prayer that not only helped me through those times but also has served me well at Mosaic ever since. Many evenings in that season of my life were spent in conversation with God while together we walked the boundary of my four-acre property. Often I would force myself to pray through the turmoil until the peace of God reigned in my heart. Sometimes it would take just a few minutes; on other occasions it would take hours before I could rest assured. My prayer times always ended with the same reassuring words accompanied by God's peace: "Trust me." And so with each confirming time of prayer, I became more resolved to let go of my own life, my own wants and needs, for the privilege of following him into the unknown. And to this day I can honestly say that I have never regretted walking away from all that I had, to discover all that I have now in Christ and the work to which I have been called these past eight years.

In a similar way, you will need to wrestle through many personal questions in prayer and in the end decide whether you too are called and willing to follow. Are you willing to leave all that is familiar to embrace what is unknown, trading your places of comfort for a life and work that is in so many ways quite uncomfortable?

The pursuit of ethnic blends will cost you real dollars and possessions. It will cost you the energy expended in exhausting physical labor; it will cost you emotionally as you serve those in need or as you learn to love others who are different from you. It may cost you your time as you spend hours in prayer too deep for words, seeking relief from the intangible, unrelenting burdens of ministry. And it will likely cost you some of your close friendships and affect your reputation among "your people." But I wouldn't trade my decision to walk, work, and worship God together with so many others who are different from me in and through Mosaic for all the riches of this world!

Given these personal challenges, why would anyone chase the multi-ethnic dream? There is really only one reason: if the kingdom of heaven is not segregated, the church on earth should not be either! That's why, in these days of increasing diversity and opportunity, we believe that local church pastors, planters, and reformers must embrace the New Testament vision of the multi-ethnic church for the sake of the gospel. Without a solid grasp of God's vision for the church, it will be difficult to face the personal challenges and opposition to your ministry.

CONCLUSION

In this chapter, we have explored some of the personal challenges you will face and emotional obstacles that must be overcome in establishing a multi-ethnic church. Yet of all that we've discussed, there are none so hard to deal with as those that impact your family in profoundly personal ways. The decision to lead a multi-ethnic church, or to attend one, for that matter, will require consideration of needs, desires, and possibilities affecting your children's present and future, issues that not many in churches today are willing or otherwise required to be concerned with.

For instance, a diverse local church quite naturally breeds a diverse student ministry. So how will you feel or what might you say if your daughter comes home one day desiring to date a young man of a different ethnicity or limited economic means? Or — as some may erroneously feel, "worse yet" — what if they want to marry cross-culturally? On another note, will you as a multi-ethnic church planter or reformer have the patience to endure a silent sense of guilt, that is, the feeling that you have not necessarily placed your children in an advantaged environment but rather put them in one without the latest bells and whistles, one in which classroom walls remain unpainted for lack of funds or in which kids come from homes of vastly different life experience? When you drive your family into the community rather than away from it on Sunday mornings — passing many other, more well-established churches along the way, where those you know attend in comfort — what will you say to assure a son who wonders why he can't go to church with all his friends? And when you lead your family week after week into areas of high poverty, crime, and sub-

IN HIS WAY AND TIME

Mike Leonzo, Lead Pastor
Living Water Community Church, Harrisburg, Pennsylvania

As my wife and I held our three-week-old adopted African American daughter in our arms for the very first time, little did we know that God had far greater plans than to merely give us a long-desired third child. At that moment there were no thoughts of my becoming a pastor or of our family starting a church—let alone a multi-ethnic one. We were just a Caucasian professional couple with two Caucasian little boys trying to figure out how not to mess up this precious little girl we were now holding.

What a difference four years makes. As our little girl was learning her ABCs, I was completing the transition from product manager to church-planting pastor. Armed with my newly earned master of divinity degree and a God-inspired vision to start a multi-ethnic church in my hometown, my wife and I began recruiting others to partner with us. There was only one problem: the only people willing to join us looked just like us.

So how do you start a multi-ethnic church with eight Caucasian families, a four-year-old African American girl, and a vision for a church that looks like the kingdom of God?

It wasn't easy. Although everything about us screamed multi-ethnic—our purpose statement, our publications, our website, our location—the one thing that was not multi-ethnic was our people. For the first several years, I passionately preached to a predominately Caucasian congregation with a small representation of people from other ethnicities. It was discouraging, but I knew with every fiber of my being that God had called me to pastor a multi-ethnic church.

So what changed to bring us to the point where we are today?

I did.

One Sunday morning, I looked into our fledgling children's program and realized that God was fulfilling the vision he had given me, but not in the way I desired. I was looking for an auditorium filled with a diverse group of adults, and that was simply not happening. But as I peered into our overflowing nursery and children's classrooms, I realized that they were filled with a diverse group of children. There were African American babies who had been adopted, biracial children born to Caucasian single moms, and Latino little boys who were being brought by their next-door neighbor. My long-sought-after diversity was happening, not with adults but with children. Suddenly I realized that God was fulfilling the vision in his way and in his time, and not necessarily in a way I had planned.

Sadly, I had forgotten that the vision of multi-ethnic ministry was not mine; it was God's. And because it was his vision, he could bring it to

cont.

pass any way that he wanted to. How could I have forgotten: "In his heart a man plans his course, but the LORD determines his steps" (Prov. 16:9).

With a dose of humility and a sense of newfound gratitude, I began to thank God for what he was actually doing and not complain to him about what I perceived he was not. It is truly amazing what fully surrendering oneself to God does. Slowly God began to bring men and women from other ethnicities who came seeking not people who looked like them but rather people who loved them.

Make no mistake about it: there is no magic formula for developing a multi-ethnic church. There is no correct ethnic mix for the planting team. But what matters most is having a heart of love for all people, a humble spirit, and an unwavering commitment to a God-ordained vision of having a local church reflect not only its community but also the kingdom of heaven.

stance abuse in spite of all that makes earthly sense, when such action weighs on your sense of significance as a father or threatens your sense of security as a mother, will you remain faithful to the calling? Will you continue to entrust yourself and your family to a faithful Creator by going where he sends and doing what he has called you to do?

Jesus once said, "Anyone who loves his father or mother more than me is not worthy of me; anyone who loves his son or daughter more than me is not worthy of me; and anyone who does not take his cross and follow me is not worthy of me" (Matt. 10:37 – 38). Hard words to understand, let alone to embrace; words we must not, however, ignore.

In the end, those who brew ethnic blends have no other choice but to remain true to the calling and to believe by faith that their families are the better for it. They have to trust that their children are learning something about God and others, about their parents and themselves, that they might never have learned in a healthy but homogeneous church or youth group. On good days and bad, we have to believe they are becoming stronger individually beyond what we see, despite that which we might fret about or feel at any given moment. Ultimately, we have to believe that in and through it all, we have well positioned our children for the future, not only to function but, more important, to contribute for Christ and kingdom in an increasingly diverse and cynical society.

And that will make it worth it all.

QUESTIONS FOR REFLECTION AND DISCUSSION

1. What is your sense of calling as it relates to your own church involvement at this time? What is your sense of what God might be saying to you about attending, planting, or pastoring a multi-ethnic church in the near future?

2. What are your assumptions about a multi-ethnic church? How certain are you that these assumptions are correct? Are these informed by Scripture or by something else?

3. Concerning your current church involvement, how much faith does it take for you to attend, serve, or pastor there? How comfortable are you currently in that environment? Is this a good thing or a bad thing? Explain your answer.

4. What excites you about your current involvement in a multi-ethnic church or about the possibility of involvement in the near future? What fears or concerns might you have as you imagine yourself and/or your family involved in such a church?

5. What key thought, revelation, or insight will you take away from this chapter? What is God asking you to do in response?

Chapter 3

HARVESTING TIPS FROM THE OLD COUNTRY

Overcoming the Theological Obstacles

> God is spirit, and his worshipers must worship in spirit and in truth.
>
> — *John 4:24*

"SHOULD I DO THIS?"

After five months of weekly meetings with the emerging church but still prior to its public birth, Amer Chami became the first person to respond to our witness of Christlike love for all people. Amer arrived in the United States from Saudi Arabia just one month before the tragic events of September 11, 2001, so his conversion was all the more miraculous on the night of Mosaic's first communion service. It was a vivid testimony to the power of unity in advancing the gospel even among the most entrenched of Muslim believers. Yet it also presented the first theological challenge I would face in pursuit of ethnic blends.

As a young man, Amer had two hopes in his mind. One was to visit a church someday to observe how Christians worship and to discover what, if any, joy they might have in doing so. The other was to convert as many people to Islam as he could.

Not long after enrolling in the University of Central Arkansas in Conway, Amer was invited to a meeting with international students, where he was introduced to a young man named Philip Lamar. A gifted evangelist, Philip had been the first to join the emerging staff of Mosaic and was eager to help internationals with their needs. To help Amer learn English, Philip began reading the Bible with him, and soon Amer was drawn to the truth of God's Word. In its pages he found a God who loved and accepted him for who he was and not for what he might accomplish with his life.

Soon Amer began attending Mosaic and discovered a community of faith that reflected the unconditional love of God for all people. Within a few months he wanted to believe as we did, but counting the cost, he was afraid of what this might mean for his life, for his family, and for his future. Seeking to resolve the tension, he prayed one day, "Dear Jesus, I believe that you are real. If you want me to follow you, please show yourself to me." At the time, he was still unsure of Christ's existence and furthermore thought that even if Jesus was God, "he would certainly not reveal himself to someone like me." If Christ failed to appear in response to his prayer, Amer reasoned, he would have a legitimate excuse not to follow his heart in the matter. He could then go on with his life, without Christ.

That same night, the first night on which we had purposed to celebrate communion at Mosaic, we had decorated the small sanctuary with candles; they were everywhere! There were candles in every stained-glass windowsill, candles in the two candelabras underneath the Advent wreaths on either side of the altar, and candles on the beautifully decorated communion table, next to baskets of bread and goblets of wine. Following the message that evening, I invited the seventy-five or so people in attendance to walk the aisle, come to the table, and receive the communion elements.[1] And the ensuing procession moved me to tears: a diverse collection of people walking down the aisle together as one to celebrate the broken body and shed blood of Christ that made it all possible — the rich with the poor, the black and the white, the deaf and disabled, Americans and internationals alike. It was a wonderful sight to behold.

When the last person had returned to his seat, I stood to close in prayer. Placing my hands on the table in front of me, I slowly lifted my head to address the congregation. Just as I was about to pray, I was surprised to see Amer standing on the other side of the table, his eyes staring intently into mine.

"Mark, is this for me? Should I do this?" he said, in his thick Middle Eastern accent, and in an instant, everything I knew to be true theologically concerning the Lord's Supper was practically challenged. I knew what I should say, but somehow I was afraid to say it. You see, I felt like saying yes to Amer so he would in no way feel excluded from the celebration. I did not want to offend him or potentially turn him away from Christ or the church. The fact is, Amer was well-known to many in the congregation and had become somewhat of a celebrity in our midst. I reasoned that if I allowed him to take communion, he would perhaps put his faith in Christ. And even if he didn't, Amer might still help us declare the vision of our church by his continued presence in our congregation. Surely God would understand my rationale! For many reasons, then, I was afraid that in saying no, I might turn him away for good.

Fortunately, I fought off my fears and held true to my convictions.

"Well, not really, Amer," I said. "Communion is reserved for those who have put their faith in Christ."

However, I didn't stop there. Prompted by the Holy Spirit, I next heard myself say, "But who knows, bro' ... maybe now's your moment. Maybe right now you would like to give your life to Jesus Christ."

Pausing momentarily, Amer asked, "If I do, must we tell anyone?" It was right then that I realized his dilemma. In saying yes to Christ, he would be putting his own life at risk, as well as the life of his dear mother and family back home. As a Muslim converting to Christianity, he could never return to the Middle East without fear of consequence. His employer would cut off his college funding and the promise of a good job upon his return. Indeed, saying yes to Christ would cost Amer all that he had, everything he knew, and, more important, everyone he loved.

After a long pause, then, and with the whole church watching, praying, and weeping behind him, Amer asked Jesus to be his Lord and Savior. And as we embraced, heads bowed together in prayer, his tears and mine fell softly on the bread and into the cup of wine on the table below. After leading him in prayer, I served him communion, and for the first time our new brother proclaimed his faith in Christ.

What prompted Amer to come forward that night? I'll let him tell you in his own words: "That evening, a bright light appeared to me during the communion service — a light I realized that only I could see. And in my heart I recognized the light to be Jesus, though I had never before this time heard him described as the Light of the World. Jesus appeared to me in answer to my prayer. I can tell you, in that moment I was no longer afraid of following him by faith. I was afraid of not doing so!"

In all my life and ministry, I had never once seen someone come to Christ at the communion table, let alone a Muslim! It was early evidence to those of us who witnessed Amer's salvation that the power of God uniquely manifests itself in the midst of unity. It's a power the people of Mosaic continue to experience to this day.

I share this story not just as an example of what God has done at Mosaic but also to point out that theological challenges are a regular part of multi-ethnic ministry. As Amer stood at the table that night, I was tempted to compromise conviction for the sake of diversity. In other ways too, and through a variety of circumstances, theological concerns will challenge you at points to clearly define just what you and your church believe. Let's take a moment to further consider theological obstacles you will have to overcome in order to build a healthy multi-ethnic church.

MANDATE OR OPTION?

As mentioned in the introduction, the homogeneous unit principle (HUP) is promoted as a pragmatic guide for planting or replicating churches that target individual people groups or certain segments of society. More specifically, it's promoted as a way for churches to grow quickly, and it has proven to be quite successful in its application. But it begs the question, Should rapid numerical growth be so prominently upheld as the standard of a church's success? Certainly, I value the effort of every well-meaning church planter and pastor, missionary and movement leader alike who is attempting to reach as many people with the gospel as possible in his or her lifetime. But I would argue that the primary question should not be, How fast can we grow a church? Rather, it should be, How can we grow a church biblically?

I believe that the HUP is a valid strategy for evangelism, but a strategy misapplied to the local church. If the goal is to evangelize, then by all means target a people group and provide them with the Word of God in their own language. Sing to them in a musical genre they understand, and become incarnate in their culture so that the gospel is expressed through customs, mores, and traditions they readily embrace. But things change once you commit yourself to establishing a local church. You are no longer at liberty to create a congregation of exclusive worshipers — that's just not a biblical option. According to Paul, the mystery of Christ is "that through the gospel the Gentiles are heirs together with Israel, *members together of one body, and sharers together in the promise in Christ Jesus*" (Eph. 3:6, emphasis mine). Make no mistake: the context in which Paul is writing makes it clear that the "one body" he is talking about is a local church. In other words, "His [Christ's] intent [is] that now, *through the church*, the manifold wisdom of God should be made known to the rulers and authorities in the heavenly realms" (Eph. 3:10, emphasis mine).

In this critical passage, Paul explains that it is God's intention for the local church to reflect the Father's love for all people — on earth as it is in heaven — through members who love one another beyond the distinctions of this world that so often and otherwise divide. Through the unity and diversity of the church, we are uniquely able, "*together with all the saints,* to grasp how wide and long and high and deep is the love of Christ" (Eph. 3:18, emphasis mine). And as we walk worthy of this calling, "to him [will] be glory *in the church* and in Christ Jesus throughout all generations, for ever and ever" (Eph. 3:21, emphasis mine).

Let me be perfectly clear on this point. I'm not arguing against those who would extend the love of God (the gospel) to people with a similar background. Rather, I am suggesting that nowhere in the New Testament will you find the apostle Paul or anyone else encouraging you to plant or develop a church that is focused on a single people group! Of course, planting a homogeneous church is something we more readily understand — and something that is much easier to do. Compared with multi-ethnic ministry, it can be a more comfortable experience for everyone involved. But it is not a question of what we want or what makes us comfortable. Christ expects us to align ourselves, and our churches, with his agenda; anything less is unacceptable. In the future, then, I believe we will all need to grow increasingly comfortable with being uncomfortable in order to be more biblical in this regard.

Prepare yourself for this theological discussion by studying relevant Scriptures, and be ready to respond with grace to all those who challenge your understanding of the HUP. Some people will try to convince you that the multi-ethnic vision is not God's *only* plan for the church but simply one option. Still others will seek to discourage your efforts by wrongly interpreting your passion for the multi-ethnic church as a critique of their own segregated congregation. Such people will challenge your enthusiasm and your calling, much as Sanballat, Tobiah, and Geshem did in approaching Nehemiah. "They were all trying to frighten us," Nehemiah recounts, "thinking, 'Their hands will get too weak for the work, and it will not be completed.' But I prayed, 'Now strengthen my hands'" (Neh. 6:9). When you encounter such people, you too should pray, "Lord, strengthen my hands" and press on in pursuit of the vision God has given you.

A MORE EXCELLENT WAY

Years ago my wife, Linda, and I (Mark) purchased a Honda Odyssey from a local dealer at a time when these vans were still fairly new to the market. Once we left the lot, however, it felt like they were everywhere! Maybe you've had a similar experience, buying something new and suddenly seeing it everywhere you go.

Likewise, once you recognize the biblical truth about the multi-ethnic nature of the New Testament local church, you will find it impossible to ignore as you read Scripture, particularly in passages concerning the life, ministry, and message of Paul, as well as in his writings. Indeed, the book of Ephesians is not the only place in the New Testament where Paul promotes the power of love to unite diverse people as one in Christ in the local church. Once you "understand [Paul's] insight into the mystery of Christ" (Eph. 3:4), if you'll look close enough, you will see him speaking of it even in places where you may not have otherwise recognized him speaking of it before. Before going on, then, let me show you one such place of theological interest concerning the multi-ethnic church: 1 Corinthians 13.

Regarding the placement of this timeless treatise on love, have you ever asked yourself the question, Why here, why now? What's its purpose, sandwiched as it is between chapters 12 and 14, which speak to the use and nature of spiritual gifts within the body?

Of course, the short answer is that spiritual gifts employed in the absence of love become "a resounding gong or a clanging cymbal" (1 Cor. 13:1). And this is certainly a valid point. Yet is there something more, something else on Paul's mind as well?

To get at this, keep in mind the apostle's words at the end of chapter 12: "But earnestly desire the greater gifts. And I will show you a still more excellent way" (1 Cor. 12:31 NASB). Sure, he has discussed spiritual gifts throughout the chapter, and he concludes by rebuking the congregation for pursuing the ones that were more "showy." The idea in the text is that their pursuit of these gifts was the result of immaturity, and Paul uses both irony and sarcasm to correct them.

Now, for a long time Bible scholars have translated the Greek word *zeloo* (meaning "to earnestly desire") as an imperative (a command). Yet the word can be either an imperative or an indicative (a statement of fact). Here, it is in fact a present active indicative verb (not an imperative one), and the context of chapters 12 through 14 supports this. Paul here is simply stating a fact — "You all are wrongly pursuing the more showy gifts!" — and not commanding the Corinthians to selfishly seek after them, that is, to seek those gifts that seem to bring more honor or attention to the individual. The fact is, he'll be back to these considerations in a moment (1 Cor. 14:1ff.). However, at this point, he wants to speak to something altogether different — as he says, to show the Corinthians "a still [in addition to gifts] more excellent way" (1 Cor. 12:31 NASB).[2]

This, then, is the purpose of chapter 13, the "something else" on Paul's mind, which begs the question, A more excellent way for what?

I believe Paul wrote chapter 13 to show his readers a more excellent way to be one in the church for the sake of the gospel. It is to manifest and model authentic love for one another (1 Cor. 13:13). Indeed, loving one another — beyond the distinctions of this world that so often and otherwise divide — is the most powerful way to express the reality, presence, and blessing of God's love before a lost and dying world. Paul wants us all to understand that the way of love is much more than a feeling. Rather, it is a path for the church to follow, a mindset for the church to embrace (1 Cor. 14:1). We are to express genuine love for every member of the body, even the ones who may seem "unpresentable" to us (1 Cor. 12:23) and at times stretch us beyond our own preferences or personalities. In fact, closer examination of the text reveals that Paul had the same thoughts in mind in here (1 Cor. 12 – 14) that he did when he penned Ephesians 3 – 4, a passage where he urges members of another multi-ethnic church of the New Testament "to live a life worthy of the calling you have received" (Eph. 4:1). Let me tell you why.

If you'll look closely, Paul's thoughts in 1 Corinthians 12 – 14 virtually parallel his thoughts in Ephesians 4. Remember, it is the same man addressing a similar church, with the same message of faith, hope, and love, all for the sake of the gospel. Through the unity of diverse believers pursuing Christ as one, he tells both churches, the world would see an authentic expression of God's love for all people … and believe![3]

To be clear, the more excellent way Paul has in mind for the church is the way of love beyond the mere exercising of gifts. Yes, it's this visible, tangible unity in Christ that will provide a more credible witness of the gospel before a world that Christ came to seek and to save (John 17:3 – 4, 23).

And why, by the way, is love the greatest of "these three" — faith, hope, and love — the three that remain (1 Cor. 13:13)?

It's simple: love is eternal.

You see, in heaven there will be no need for faith or hope. Faith and hope are things we exercise on earth, yet God *is* and *will forever be* love. Therefore, it is unconditional, eternal love that he would have us exemplify, as well, and express to one another, on earth as it is in heaven, beyond race or class distinctions. And when such love is displayed — in and through the local church — we will win the lost and skeptical for Christ. It is love that is the more excellent way and that is required to brew ethnic blends!

A WAY OR THE WAY?

Creating a healthy multi-ethnic church will often require you, as a leader, to accommodate expressions of faith and worship beyond your own personal experience or preference. To be clear, I am not suggesting that you accommodate divergent or heretical theology. Rather, get comfortable in accommodating requests from members that promote a spirit of inclusion within the congregation, especially requests that may challenge you to go beyond your comfort zone. Failing to value the perspectives of others can be a costly mistake.

I once knew a white pastor who, in the early days of his ministry, refused to hold funerals in the church facility. He would allow memorial services, but he refused to allow bodies or caskets into the sanctuary. When I asked him why he held this opinion, he told me that it was because of his belief that "the life of a Christian should be celebrated and not mourned in death." He saw this as a way of emphasizing that the departed was no longer with us on earth but, in that moment, wonderfully alive in heaven. Of course, his beliefs were all rooted in Scripture. The problem was not with his theology, however, but with how he was applying it in the church.

JUST DO IT

David Nelms, Senior/Lead Pastor
Grace Fellowship, West Palm Beach, Florida

I remember singing as a child, "Jesus loves the little children, all the children of the world. Red and yellow, black and white, they are precious in his sight. Jesus loves the little children of the world."

I didn't sing it very well, but I believed what I sang; it just made sense to me that God cared for all races. Since he made us all and since his Son died for all, it made sense to me that God cared for his entire creation: all races, all faces, all places! But if that was so, why didn't we love them too?

We said that we did. We talked about our love for the world. We even gave extra money to send out missionaries throughout the world to reach people for Christ. We cared about the Mexican, as long as he was in Mexico, and we cared about the African, as long as she was in Africa. But if we loved the Mexican and the African enough to send missionaries to reach them *over there*, shouldn't we love them enough to open up our church doors and reach out to them *over here*?

The more I read my Bible, the more I realized that all people matter to God. Black people. White people. Brown people. People who are rich and people who are poor. Good people, bad people, males and females. Yes, all people matter to God. And if they matter to God, they ought to matter to us. Our arms should be opened wide to them, and they should be more than welcome in our fellowship. They should be wanted and valued!

From the Scriptures, I discovered we would not find a "white church" or a "black church" in heaven. What we will find is a great, called-out assembly of Christ worshipers, gathered around the throne and praising him as one unified body. If that is God's plan

A sizeable contingent of African Americans who had been otherwise attracted to his church soon took exception with the pastor's policy. For when one of their own died — a respected leader in the community — they were considerably hurt when the pastor refused to allow the funeral to take place in the church facility. Not only were the members of his church confused, but also other African Americans outside the church soon began to disparage the ministry and to say of him, "Some pastor! The man will take your money in life but will not stand with you in death!"

When the pastor learned of the growing controversy, he made an important decision. He invited the African American members

for eternity, wouldn't he be pleased if we moved in that direction now!

Soon I began seeing the nations everywhere in the Bible. In Genesis, I read about Abraham's seed blessing all people everywhere. In Psalms, I read, "Let the nations praise him, let all the nations praise him." The Prophets told me the day would come when the knowledge of the Lord would cover the earth like the oceans. In the Gospels, I read, "For God so loved the world ..." The Epistles declared that the gospel was sent "to the Jew first, but also to the Greek." And in Revelation, I read with excitement about a day coming when a multitude from every people group on earth will gather around God's throne to worship him together as one, a multitude so large that they cannot be counted! By contrast, as I looked around our own congregation, I saw only people who looked like me. I felt sorrow and conviction. So I repented and decided that if the nations matter to God, they would matter to us too!

We are not a perfect congregation. And yes, there are many challenges that come with being a church for all nations. But there's a whole lot of joy as well! There's nothing like looking out over a congregation from eighty or ninety countries and watching as they praise God together, wash each other's feet, serve communion to each other, and kneel at the altar to pray for and with one another. What a testimony of God's love for all people, to see black, white, Latino, and Asian members embracing each other and loving one another, brothers and sisters in Christ and in our church.

So how do you grow a multi-ethnic church? It's simple. You just read the Bible and do what it says!

of his church to meet with him privately as a group. In the meeting, he acknowledged that his thinking was merely preferential and was not at all imposed by the Bible. He then asked for their forgiveness and assured them that in the future he would accommodate such funeral requests by members of his congregation. And to their credit, the entire group accepted his apology and chose to remain in his church.

The fact is, much of what passes for religious doctrine or practical theology in our churches today is personal, preferential, or culturally bound. With this in mind, multi-ethnic church leaders must be able to recognize the differences. The ability to accommodate various forms of evangelical faith and worship without compromising doctrinal beliefs is an essential characteristic of those who would successfully brew ethnic blends. To do so, we must recognize that our way is only *a* way and not necessarily *the* way (in terms of right or wrong) to view or to do something in a church filled with people who are not like us.

SPIRIT AND TRUTH

Through the years, we have found that some who join our fellowship go through a period of theological adjustment in which they find themselves wrestling with one or more points of doctrine that are not defined (one way or the other) or emphasized by the church. Otherwise loving Mosaic, these people may experience a time of spiritual or personal uncertainty in which they find themselves compelled to reevaluate positions they have previously assumed to be true or have been taught were essential to their faith and practice in another congregation. We believe that it is important for them to wrestle through these issues in order to move forward as one with the church in spirit and truth. And in times when people are struggling with such issues, it is the responsibility of multi-ethnic church leaders to gently guide them away from extremes to embrace a more balanced center in Christ. In order to do so, you will need to exercise both wisdom and theological depth.

To exercise wisdom in these situations will require you to evaluate specific questions, concerns, or situations according to their own unique merits while avoiding generalities. In other words, the antithesis of wisdom is legalism. Legalism requires that we apply the same set of rules to every condition and person regardless of circumstance. But this is a recipe for disaster in a multi-ethnic church. Pastors who exercise wisdom attend to both the letter of the law and the spirit of the law when giving counsel and should be prepared to address diverse concerns with sensitivity *and* theological depth. Pat or naive answers do not take into account an individual's background, experience, or reason for coming forward with a theological question. And this understanding too you must acquire to address confusion or avoid compromise within the body.

Early in our ministry, we were challenged theologically concerning our approach to the season of Lent. More specifically, there were concerns about our sponsorship of an annual Ash Wednesday service at Mosaic. Many of these concerns came from our Hispanic and Latino members, who in many cases had come to Christ from an aberrant form of Catholicism as practiced in some parts of Central and South America. In their minds, anything remotely Catholic could not be considered Christian, and they did not believe that such practices should be part of an evangelical church. In particular, they called into question the Ash Wednesday service and our use of ash to mark the foreheads of believers as an outward sign of inner repentance.

When we became aware of the issues swirling in our midst, we began by explaining ourselves, hoping that the conflict would recede once people understood our position. However, our pursuit of cross-cultural competence, and our desire to accommodate differences, would not allow us to disregard their concerns entirely. In other words, we did not want to throw the baby out with the bathwater, so we sought to create a balanced perspective, one which everyone could embrace.

How did we resolve this issue? Today we still mark the beginning of Lent with an Ash Wednesday service at Mosaic. But we take great care to explain for Hispanics and Latinos what is and is not intended. Beyond this, we intentionally involve Hispanic and Latino leadership in the planning of the service and now use oil instead of ash as a symbol of the hope, healing, and happiness we have found in Christ. Such accommodation of minorities within the church in no way compromises our core convictions. Rather, it demonstrates a practical understanding of Paul's teaching in Philippians 2:4, where he admonishes members of a local church to "look not only to your own interests, but also to the interests of others." This verse serves to guide all of us at Mosaic whenever there are differences of opinion.

ACHIEVING DOCTRINAL UNITY

Of course, in any church, it is important to clarify what you believe. But for those pursuing the multi-ethnic church, it is essential. For with diverse people comes diverse theology; consequently, multi-ethnic church leaders must be up-front and clear about the beliefs of the church in order to "keep the unity of the Spirit through the bond of peace" (Eph. 4:3). We should never compromise our convictions for the sake of diversity.

One way to be proactive in this regard is to post a doctrinal statement on your website or in some other visible location within the church. I recommend, however, that it speak only about the essential doctrines of the Christian faith, allowing room to accommodate various views on the more nonessential positions of teaching that you will certainly encounter from those seeking to join a multi-ethnic church. Resist the urge to speak to every possible issue in your doctrinal statement, and beyond this, do not be afraid of divergent opinions concerning the nonessentials. As long as those who hold them do not become divisive — by seeking to impose their views on others or by failing to consider others as more important than themselves in the practice of their faith — the healthy dialogue and the exchange of experiential understanding will invite and inspire spiritual growth within the body.

Your doctrinal statement might also address specific topics as they surface, or attitudes that should be present, in a congregation seeking to walk, work, and worship God together as one. For instance, Mosaic's own doctrinal statement concludes with the following phrases:

- We believe that the prayer of Jesus Christ (John 17) declares unity among believers to be the greatest expression of God's love for the world and the greatest witness to it of the fact that he himself is Messiah.
- We believe that the pattern of the New Testament local church reflects this unity and that in these churches, people of various ethnicities and economic means pursued God together as one.
- We believe that the kingdom of heaven is not segregated along ethnic and economic lines.
- We believe that local churches on earth should not be either.

By maintaining a doctrinal statement that is simple yet substantive, one that addresses only the core tenets of the Christian faith, we have been able to establish theological unity within the body while still allowing room for diverse opinions on a wide range of spiritual, philosophical, or sociopolitical topics.

CONSIDERATION WITHOUT COMPROMISE

New members of Mosaic come to us not only from a variety of ethnic and economical backgrounds but also from a variety of theological and denominational experiences: from knowing absolutely nothing about Christ to coming from mainline Protestant, evangelical, and nondenominational churches. Our membership includes people of Catholic, Pentecostal, charismatic, and fundamentalist origin; they are Arminian, Reformed, and everything in between. Because we attract such a wide spectrum of theological views, most of the time the discussion revolves around questions or concerns about matters that are (for us) of secondary doctrinal importance. For example, individuals may press us to declare the precise timing of the rapture, the proper mode of baptism, or the true manner of one's salvation. Often, they will state their own positions as absolute truth, or will want us to express biblical certainty on a point where we believe none exists. Adding to the complexity, we often find ourselves agreeing with many but not all of their assertions!

Effectively navigating the theological diversity of multi-ethnic ministry will require more of you than mere knowledge of Scripture. Like a seesaw functioning in perfect equilibrium, you too will need to maintain a precarious balance of "consideration without compromise," coupled with a steady mix of awareness, effort, and instinct. It can be all too easy at times to express a polarized opinion or to come across as too dogmatic in a careless moment of conversation with someone who is not at all like you who has a different theological background or a different understanding of a particular issue.

Having said this, we are not afraid to address specific theological concerns outside the scope of our formal doctrinal statement. As the need arises, we have frequently taken the time to clearly state what the church believes about a given issue, by writing a position paper. These papers provide further clarification of our beliefs and address corporate thinking on topics such as election versus free will, the local church, and homosexuality. In these papers, our responses are governed by the belief that godly wisdom is most often dispensed from a well-balanced and biblically grounded center of understanding.[4]

With this in mind, let me provide you with three examples of the types of theological issues we have had to address through position papers in consideration, without compromise, of people seeking to join the unity and diversity of Mosaic.

1. Eternal Security

The doctrine of eternal security (or assurance of salvation/justification) states that following genuine repentance, it is impossible for a believer to lose his or her salvation. In other words, from the moment of conversion by faith, believers in Christ are eternally secure and destined for heaven. At Mosaic we hold to this position; it is presumed in our doctrinal statement and more specifically addressed in one of our position papers. Nevertheless, a good number of people have come to us over time believing something different, and a few have even found their way into leadership before recognizing the discrepancy. In most instances, these have been taught that only when faith is exercised consistently through obedience and demonstrated through good works can one have hope of a heavenly fate.

In addressing questions on this subject through the years, we have seen three outcomes. Some have come to understand and embrace our position, having never considered an alternative point of view. Others, though, after learning of our beliefs, have removed themselves not only from positions of leadership but also from the church, feeling that they could not teach or accept this doctrine in good conscience. Another couple's ongoing struggle with the doctrine, however, provides a third, equally palatable possibility.

Ronald and Barbara Young spent years in the Church of Christ before coming to our church, and for much of that time Ronald served as a pastor within the denomination. Given the strength of their faith, character, and experience, it was not long before this husband-and-wife team began to make a difference at Mosaic. As newly appointed leaders, Ronald and Barbara established a name tag ministry within the church, whereby on Sunday mornings we can now greet one another by name, track attendance, and use the information to follow up with those we have not seen in a while. In addition, they put together two classes for those interested in membership and trained a team to teach each class.

Like others before them, however, Ronald and Barbara came to Mosaic not believing in the doctrine of eternal security. To get a better understanding of our beliefs, they tried to approach the issue with an open mind and came to speak to the leadership of the church, genuinely seeking truth. While they have come to understand our position, still to this day they are not entirely settled in their beliefs on the subject. Perhaps, as we've agreed, our differences are only a matter of emphasis and the way things are communicated. For what they reject is not so much the doctrine of eternal security as the idea that one can simply utter words of truth he or she does not really understand, believe, or embrace and somehow be saved. And we agree with them on that point. With this common ground, then, we are able to move forward in our ministry together, having communicated respectfully about our differences. As a volunteer leader, Ronald is careful not to contradict the corporate teaching on the subject, and as directional leader, I seek to ensure a clear, authentic presentation of the gospel in all that is said and done through the church.

2. Speaking in Tongues

Maybe, like us, you've been asked this question at your church: When a person speaks or prays in church in a language other than English, is he or she speaking in tongues? Don't laugh! We've had to address this question on more than one occasion, and in multiethnic ministry it's likely that you will too. In addition, some have wondered whether an interpreter must be provided for those speaking in Spanish, for example, in order to uphold the integrity and intent of Paul's teaching in 1 Corinthians 14:6–17. How would you answer?

After biblical study of this issue, we believe that earthly languages invented by human beings are not at all the same (in kind or purpose) as those distributed spiritually as a gift by the Holy Spirit. And clearly, it is the *spiritual* gift of tongues that Paul is addressing in 1 Corinthians 14, as he does previously in 1 Corinthians 12. So the answer to the first question is no: when a Hispanic, for instance, prays in Spanish in the church, he or she is not speaking in tongues, per se. Incidentally, when people pray at Mosaic, we encourage them to pray in their first (heart) language, whether or not they can or feel the need to translate for the predominately English-speaking congregation.

But that brings us to the second question. Doesn't Paul state that words spoken in the church should be understood so as to edify and instruct those who hear (1 Cor. 14:17, 19)? Yes, the principle is true, but we have found that there is more than one way to edify or instruct others through language in the church. At Mosaic, for example, we have often been edified through the passion of Nigerians praying in the Yoruba language of West Africa or by our brother Cesar Ortega praying in the Spanish language of Honduras. In such times, these too welcome the opportunity to express themselves more freely to God in their heart languages. Such prayers in languages other than English also instruct the rest of us, for in and through them we are reminded that the God we worship is not just the God of English speakers. The fact is, he is the God of the whole earth, the One who understands the cries of every man and woman, no matter who they are, where they come from, or what language they speak.

And while we are on the topic of praying in tongues, I should also note that there are some within our body who pray in tongues and others who do not. Most of those who practice this gift do so in the context of private prayer, as Paul discusses in 1 Corinthians 14:4, 18 – 19. Yet on occasion, during a worship service or in a corporate time of prayer, you may hear some people praying discreetly in tongues to the Lord. If such praying were to become disruptive to the service, we would speak to the individual and encourage sensitivity to the larger body, based on Philippians 2:3 – 4.

3. Women in Ministry

In light of Mosaic's commitment to diversity, we are often asked to share our views concerning the role of women in leadership, and of course in every church this is a valid question. Yet I have found that some who ask it of us have a broader agenda in mind—namely to link one commitment to the other. In other words, the question can sometimes carry with it the assumption that a commitment to ethnic and economic diversity requires a commitment to unlimited opportunities for women in all roles of leadership within the church and, more specifically, ministering from the pulpit or as a member of the governing board. As you might expect, some believe that these two issues are indelibly linked; others believe that they are not, and that each issue must be examined biblically, independently, of the other. In the end, this is a question you will have to settle for yourself.

What I can tell you is that your conclusions on these matters likely will hinge on your understanding and interpretation of two key passages in the Bible: 1 Timothy 3:1–11 and Galatians 3:26–29.

Of course, conservative theologians and pastors have for quite some time referenced the 1 Timothy passage in reserving the office of elder for men only. These ministry leaders maintain that Paul instructs Timothy to appoint male elders, and that Paul considers it the sole responsibility of qualified men to exercise spiritual authority "over" the body. Very often, this understanding informs a gender-exclusive pulpit as well.

However, an argument can be made from the Galatians passage that Paul's gender-specific teaching in 1 Timothy, concerning the appointment of male elders, is not intended by God to be a "timeless truth" to govern churches in the future but rather is, interpretively, culture-bound. Those who espouse this view will consider Paul's teaching in the Galatians passage concerning the oneness of all believers in Christ—beyond the distinctions of race, class, and gender—a superseding principle that should inform our thinking on the subject today, in a Western society in which women are no longer limited to roles and responsibilities traditionally reserved for men.

Having briefly framed the debate, I say again that this is a question you will have to settle for yourself. So, what do you believe?

JUSTICE AND JESUS

Before concluding this chapter, let me add a brief word about the very good and growing concern for social justice and community transformation among evangelical Christians and churches. For some, this is nothing new, as they've been proactive in addressing such concerns for quite some time. Indeed many of these people and churches, long ago, established 501(c)(3) Community Development Corporations (CCDs) through which they could address a host of needs within their communities, like the need for early childhood and character development, the need for educational tutoring, the need for health care and housing among low-income families and the homeless. More recently, some churches concerned with social justice and community transformation have been described as "externally focused" in their efforts to address the physical and material needs of local schools, to honor public servants, or to develop community spaces. In fact, Leadership Network has a leadership community devoted to the growth of this movement. Still, other churches seeking to impact the community just outside their doors will identify themselves as "missional."

No matter the label, I want to make two points drawn from a proper theological perspective.

First, we have found that in a healthy multi-ethnic church, social justice is not so much a program to pursue; rather, it is who we are. In other words, a missional mindset quite naturally flows from the diversity of the body itself. In this sense, then, Mosaic is not so much focused on becoming missional; rather we are the mission! We are not so much focused on building bridges to the community; we are the community! Indeed, we recognize that community transformation stems first and foremost from a community in transformation, and that is what we are: a multi-ethnic and economically diverse community of people being transformed through the blood of Christ, learning to walk, work, and worship God together as one in and through the local church (see Eph. 2:11–22).

In addition, we must recognize that social justice and community transformation cannot be realized, or sustained, if we who champion justice do not also champion Jesus. For no amount of advocation, education, or legislation can ultimately satisfy people's need for salvation in Christ. My point is this: in our zeal for justice we must also be zealous for Jesus.

Recently, I was discussing such things with Chris Rice, codirector of the Center for Reconciliation at Duke Divinity School in Durham, North Carolina, and he agrees.[5] Chris is a forerunner in the multiethnic church movement and is widely respected as an authority on the subject of reconciliation. In fact, in a recent blog post, Chris wrote,

> At the annual Christian Community Development Association (CCDA) conference in 2009, three thousand people packed the room. Unlikely co-founder John Perkins, now nearly eighty years old and the son of a Mississippi sharecropper, was teaching passionately from 1 John about God's love. I was struck by the fact that maybe one-third of those in attendance were under thirty years old. Most are Christians living and ministering in the abandoned places of North America, and beyond. Suddenly I ran into an old friend from Chattanooga, Carl Ellis. Carl is an African-American veteran of the days when such ministry was deeply resisted in white American evangelicalism. We marveled at the scene before us. "You know," he said, "CCDA has given evangelicals credibility in America."
>
> Yes, the Christians in the room were zealous for social justice: from those involved in a multi-million dollar church-based community development ministry like Lawndale Christian Church in Chicago, to those involved in communities of the "new monasticism," to fledgling storefront churches, to wealthy lay people and suburban congregations partnering across city divides, to a ministry whose codirector is a former drug dealer who spent time in prison.[6]

Later I discussed this blog post with Chris by phone. "Do you think that some people," I asked him, "are more passionate for justice than they are for Jesus?" Here's what he had to say: "Yes, there is a danger, in the midst of all the urgent needs and current rush to

UNSHAKABLE CONVICTION

Jonathan Seda, Senior Pastor
Grace Church, Dover, Delaware

Convinced of the biblical imperative for the multi-ethnic church, convicted by the reality that I was the pastor of a very Caucasian middle-class congregation in an ethnically diverse community, and highly motivated to do something, I set out with great enthusiasm to lead our body in pursuit of the multi-ethnic vision. As a first step, I presented the vision to our pastoral staff, and though they were initially shocked at the scope of change I was proposing, they soon came to embrace it. Next I went to the elders, and they too, after some discussion, seemed to be on board. Yet I would soon come to learn that it was only their love for and loyalty to me, their pastor of many years, that had led them to initially accept what I was suggesting. I would later learn that many of them had serious reservations. At the time, it was hard for me to discern their concerns. Certainly, some of our leaders assumed I was being influenced by political correctness.

Believing all of us were in agreement, I took our pastoral staff and elders on a retreat to begin thinking about and planning specific ways in which we might implement the multi-ethnic vision within our church. And that's when the wheels fell off the cart! On that retreat I discovered, with a sinking heart, that our leadership did *not* truly embrace the vision. I was crushed!

Only one thing sustained me in those discouraging days: an unshakable conviction that people from all backgrounds, when gathered together as one in the local church through common faith in Christ, most clearly demonstrate the reconciling power of the gospel before an unbelieving world.

And so, following the failed retreat, we began a more measured leg in our journey toward transforming a homogeneous church into a multi-ethnic one. Rather than taking any uncertain or drastic steps, we simply wrestled with the Scriptures. For the next several years, we intently studied what God had to say on the subject. Recognizing that the vision was simply too big for us to move forward without unanimity, we intentionally waited until every elder truly embraced it. In time that moment came, and for me personally it brought with it a joy and excitement I cannot fully express in words.

Looking back, I can now see that the breakthrough occurred through a simple yet profound proposal. One day I suggested that we take a map and draw a circle around our church, call that area our primary mission field (the parish), and commit ourselves to doing whatever it might take to reach the people—*all* the people—living around us. The joining of hearts around this proposal was instantly and

cont.

wonderfully evident. Some three years now have passed, and we've never looked back! We are becoming what I believe God would have us to be: a church seeking to reflect his love for all people in a tangible way.

To fellow travelers on this journey, I will say this: only a deep, unshakable commitment to the biblical mandate for the multi-ethnic church will enable you to stay the course when you feel like giving up—and believe me, you will often feel like giving up! Strong theological moorings will strengthen your resolve to press on in such times when, in the words and imagery of Christ (Matt. 7:24–27), the rain comes down and streams rise up, when shifting winds blow and beat against you. Indeed, an unshakable commitment to the biblical mandate must be established not only in your own mind and heart but also in that of your leaders and your people, no matter how long it takes. To the degree that a biblical foundation has been established, you will be able to confidently move forward with the vision, knowing that you are building a multi-ethnic church upon the solid foundation of the Word of God.

Christian activism, of losing sight of the source, story, power, and theological commitments which give our ministry its distinctive shape and goal: being centered in Christ and in Christ's gift, the church. Jesus without justice is insufficient, yet justice without Jesus is also insufficient."[7]

BY OUR LOVE

In these days, local church pastors, planters, and reformers are envisioning congregations through which men and women of diverse backgrounds can worship God together as one — evidenced, in part, by the fact that you are reading this book! Yet for dreams to become reality, it is essential that the growing fascination with the multi-ethnic church be informed by sound theological reflection. In other words, your efforts to build a healthy multi-ethnic church (indeed, the emerging movement itself) must be based on biblical truth rather than on the desire to be culturally relevant, if you are to succeed in establishing a first-century church in the twenty-first century. For, as it is written, "It is not good to have zeal without knowledge, nor to be hasty and miss the way" (Prov. 19:2).

The good news is that by applying biblical truth concerning the multi-ethnic nature of the local church — truth that has for too long been overlooked or ignored — your message and your methods will be seen as culturally relevant by a skeptical public. More than that, your church will establish credibility in an increasingly diverse and cynical society, resulting in the salvation of people "from every tribe and language and people and nation" (Rev. 5:9) — people like Amer. Yes, they'll know we are Christians by our love.

QUESTIONS FOR REFLECTION AND DISCUSSION

1. What is your understanding of the homogeneous unit principle? Do you agree with the statement that it is "a valid strategy for evangelism, but a strategy misapplied to the local church"? Why or why not?

2. What (if any) biblical passages can you cite in support of the homogeneous unit principle as it relates to church planting or development? What (if any) biblical justification is there to support the notion of church planters defining a specific target group of people to whom they will cater?

3. The authors write, "Much of what passes for religious doctrine or practical theology in our churches today is personal, preferential, or culturally bound." Do you agree or disagree with this statement? Why? Whether you agree or disagree, can you think of a case in which this is true?

4. What, in your mind, are the nonnegotiable, core tenets of the Christian faith that should be detailed in a doctrinal statement? What specific areas of Christian doctrine, in your opin-

ion, might be described as dealing with nonessential areas or topics of interest? How comfortable are you with people attending your church who hold various theological views on the nonessential issues of the Christian faith? How might this help or hinder the effort to build a healthy multi-ethnic church? Explain your answer.

5. What key thought, revelation, or insight will you take away from this chapter? What is God asking you to do in response?

Chapter 4

REGULAR OR DECAF?

Overcoming the Philosophical Obstacles

> To make plain to everyone the administration of this
> mystery ... that now, through the church, the manifold
> wisdom of God should be made known.
>
> — *Ephesians 3:9 – 10*

AS ANY LOCAL CHURCH PASTOR or planter can attest, a well-reasoned philosophy of ministry — a biblically defined, clearly articulated system of beliefs and values concerning one's approach to fulfilling the vision — is important for leaders to develop for the long-term growth and health of the congregation. However, in instances where ministry leaders are seeking to unite ethnically and economically diverse people together as one in the church, the philosophical concerns that must be addressed are often much broader in scope than those typically encountered in a homogeneous congregation.

ELECTION RESULTS

One Sunday morning in September of 2008, as a historic presidential race was heating up, I (Mark) addressed the people of Mosaic to remind them of our position on politics. In general, I reminded them that we do not allow for the promotion or endorsement of individual candidates within the church, even though we have several members who have run for office or serve as elected officials. For the sake of unity, I encouraged the congregation to check their politics at the door during the election season and to align themselves first and foremost with the Prince of Peace in all of their interaction with one another. Outside our proverbial walls, however, I encouraged them to be as actively involved in the political process as their interests or convictions might dictate. And I reminded them of our goal as leaders: to keep Christ at the center of our lives, and the church free from the influence of any loyalties we might privately grant to political candidates or specific party affiliations.

Thankfully, my words were met that day with heartfelt approval and applause. And throughout the campaign season, though many church members strongly favored one candidate or another, they never allowed their personal views to threaten their love for one another or the unity of our body.

Within a multi-ethnic church, you will find a variety of political persuasions and people who are not afraid to express their differing opinions one way or another on local, state, and national issues affecting their lives. One philosophical question you will have to address, then, is, What are we to do with politics? As this story illustrates, how you respond will either help or hinder your efforts at promoting unity and a common vision throughout the church.[1]

In addition to politics, there are other philosophical considerations you should be prepared to address in seeking to establish a healthy multi-ethnic church. Perhaps one of the most pressing questions to ask is, What are we to do with language?

MODELS OF ENGAGEMENT

In a previous chapter, I introduced you to the homogeneous unit principle (HUP), which is promoted as a means for planting or replicating churches that target individual people groups or certain segments of society, and, more specifically, as a way for churches to quickly grow. Sadly, widespread application of the HUP has led to the further segregation of the local church along ethnic and economic lines.[2] Yet some will ask, How can we overcome the many obstacles, such as language, that naturally limit the ability of diverse people to come together in and through the local church? To answer this, we'll look at three philosophical models of engagement from a characteristically North American perspective.

1. Intended Exclusion: Us and Them

Figure 6 represents the approach of well-meaning English-speaking congregations committed to the HUP and attempting to plant churches or address the spiritual needs of diverse people groups living in the community. For instance, an established English-speaking congregation might allow a fledgling Korean church to meet in their facility on Sunday afternoons whether or not the two assemblies have any other relational or denominational connection. Or an existing English-speaking congregation might launch a "Spanish church" on their own property or

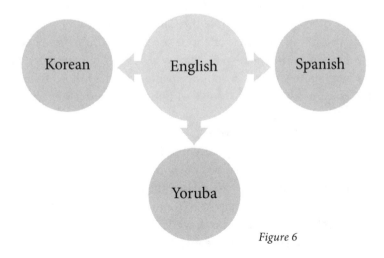

Figure 6

somewhere else in the city, even going so far as to hire a Hispanic or Latino pastor to lead the effort. Or an English-speaking congregation might decide to add an additional service for Nigerians speaking in Yoruba.

While I applaud any church willing to address the needs of diverse believers beyond themselves, this approach creates an "us and them" situation that hinders the further development of relationships between these distinct groups of people. For while the two groups may politely smile at one another on the church grounds, most will likely wonder if there is not a better way to do things. From the outset, then, we saw this model as problematic, and we determined to do things differently.

Among the first Hispanics to attend our church were two women who had come to us from a trailer park in Alexander, a small town just outside Little Rock. These women did not speak any English but came anyway, having heard of the church through a local Spanish-language publication in which we had run an advertisement. There to welcome them to Mosaic was our only other attending Hispanics at the time, a family who could speak English. The head of this home (I'll call him Julio) had experience as a preacher. Together with his wife, Julio was willing to preach to these women in Spanish, to translate for them as needed, or to help in other ways to integrate them into the life of our congregation, beginning with the worship service. Concerning the service, we decided for the next week that we would all remain together for singing, prayer, and announcements and that following this, the Hispanics would be dismissed to hear a message by Julio in their own language.

A brilliant idea, don't you agree?

So we sang — well, actually, the English-speakers sang and the Spanish-speakers clapped their hands — and with the best of intentions that day, we dismissed the four of them just before the message. Together they rose from their seats, walked up the aisle and back out of the church while the rest of us in attendance looked on and smiled. Believe me, it was pitiful to watch, and it's still painful to remember! Later that week we all agreed there had to be a better way.[3]

After further research, we concluded that the only way to fully integrate Hispanics and Latinos in the worship service — and consequently, to make them truly a part of "us" — was to provide simultaneous translation of the message over headsets. This led us to new thinking and to develop a second approach to overcoming the language obstacle.

2. Unintended Exclusion: Them in Us

Figure 7 represents our mentality throughout the first five years of Mosaic. Looking back, I realize now that we were so determined to avoid the us-and-them approach that we created an equally problematic solution I've labeled "Them in Us." This approach had its own share of problems, mainly in providing help only for those first-generation internationals (whom we

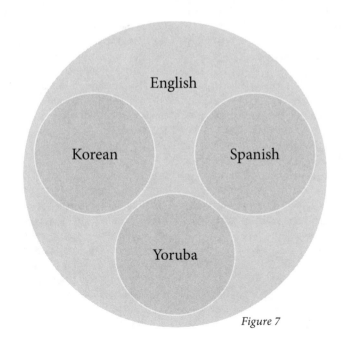

Figure 7

MORE THAN MERE TOOLS

Alejandro (Alex) Mandes, Director of Hispanic Ministries and Gateway Evangelical Free Church of America, Minneapolis, Minnesota

Many people are now looking to the year 2042, a tipping point at which time Latinos/Hispanics (L/H) will be the largest minority of the new "majority-minority" in the United States, and they are wondering how to make an impact upon this people group today.* But all too often they wrongly conclude there is little use in trying, because of the language barrier, the Catholic lock on L/H, the complexities of undocumented immigration, or the socioeconomic divide. While there is some truth to each of these obstacles, there are certainly ways to overcome them. Yet I want to speak to a more global issue.

Sometimes we put ministry tools above relationships.

I am shaped in this regard having been raised in a very large Hispanic family. Often when we gathered as family, we would rent a hall and even have our own priest come to give the blessing. Many others who were not part of our family, however, were also welcomed and accepted as one of us at such gatherings—in fact, we called them *primos* (or cousins). We always made time and room for each other, as we do even now.

When I first left my Hispanic cocoon in Laredo, Texas, I knew there were Anglos out there, because I saw them on T.V. But I was shocked upon arriving at the University of Texas in Austin, where I saw them everywhere! I had chosen to go there to continue my discipleship training within a distinguished campus ministry. Yet soon I felt like a little goldfish that had jumped out of a safe tank and was drowning in another environment. Everybody was so busy! Appointments lasted fifty-nine minutes and fifty-nine seconds or twenty-nine minutes and fifty-nine seconds exactly; decisions were made according to strategic goals; my value was decided by what I had done lately for Jesus. And worse still, it seemed that the tools of ministry were more important than the very relationships we were supposed to form for the sake of the ministry! Believe me, it was a painful time! I watched as many of my other L/H friends involved in the campus ministry did not stick around in the otherwise white-led ministry. In fact, such a trend remains all too common today.

The problem of inclusive ministry (then and now) has little to do with language, economic challenges, or any of the other generalized factors I might list. It has to do with the value (or lack thereof) we place on developing and enjoying cross-cultural relationships of mutual respect, shared responsibility, and trust. Here are a few of the principles I have tried to instill in others to promote the value of multi-ethnic relationships:

1. *Who I do something with (or for) is just as important as what I seek to do.* Fulfilling the Great Commission is not meant to be an out-of-body experience. It is simply extending the family of God. Jesus said, "I am *with* you always" (Matt. 28:20, emphasis mine). Learn to "be with" your ministry partners or with those you seek to serve.

2. *Love is a universal language; it is more than just a word.* Our love for Christ and others is observed in deeds, smiles, and touches. All of these are easily translated into Spanish without *Rosetta Stone!* Latino/Hispanic individuals are particularly apt at reading these subtle forms of communication. Don't worry if you can't speak Spanish or know very little of the language—speak the language of love.

3. *Love does in fact cover a multitude of sins.* Offenses are unavoidable. Work proactively and intentionally to fill the love bank before they arise.

4. *Anyone can be familia.* As I learned growing up, family is not always about blood. In fact, the title of the book *Three Cups of Tea* comes from a Balti proverb that might as well be a Hispanic proverb. It says, "The first time you share tea with a Balti, you are a stranger. The second time you take tea, you are an honored guest. The third time you share a cup of tea, you become family."** And I might add, after four cups of coffee, you are my family; I will die for you.

Goals, schedules, strategies, and planning are all tools in my bag, but they do not define who I am or what I believe is most important in ministry. Indeed, every culture has something wonderful to contribute in advancing the kingdom of God on earth as it is in heaven. And we must all learn to listen to and love one another across cultural divides, in a spirit of mutual respect and humility. When we take the time to truly care, we will be amazed at how much we can endure together because of loyal love. We can all be *primos* in the body of Christ!

*See Conor Dougherty, "Whites to Lose Majority Status in U.S. by 2042," Wall Street Journal, August 14, 2008, A3, *http://online.wsj.com/article/SB121867492705539109.html* (accessed September 23, 2009).

**Greg Mortenson and David Oliver Relin, *Three Cups of Tea: One Man's Mission to Promote Peace One School at a Time* (New York: Penguin, 2006), 150.

sometimes refer to as 1.0s) who were enthusiastically devoted to more immediate integration. In other words, Hispanics and Latinos who were willing to wear headsets while listening to a message simultaneously translated from English were those who highly valued immersion in North American culture. Consequently, they were willing to embrace a good bit of discomfort to be part of the church. Whether driven by personality, personal relationships, or pragmatism, these were the ones who were willing to sing songs in English (while reading Spanish lyrics italicized below each line) and to sing them in a musical style with which they were largely unfamiliar. And they were willing to encourage their children to attend Mosaic's English-speaking, age-appropriate ministries. In the end, they were eager to endure these initial difficulties and help us work through problems for the sake of the gospel and the unity of the church. Indeed, they deserve much credit, for we would certainly not be the church we are today if they had not been willing to walk patiently with us on the journey!

In those early years, however, we found that we were experiencing the same troubling problem time after time. While many first-generation Hispanics and Latinos were being led to the Lord and coming into the church, most would remain with us only for a few months. Over time a common refrain emerged whenever we would ask why these people were leaving our church: "We love the people and the heart of Mosaic," they would say, "but it is just too difficult to worship in English." The fact is, we were reluctant in those days to even allow a language-specific small group (e.g., a Spanish-speaking group) to meet, fearing that a slippery slope could develop and lead us to the very segregation we were determined to avoid. We had no idea how to adjust our principles or practices without violating the biblical mandate or our core commitments. So while many 1.0s came to us during those years, many of them left, with heartbreaking regularity, after only a few visits. And we were forced to accept it (or so we thought) as a reality of multi-ethnic ministry.

3. Graduated Inclusion: We Are One

By 2006 we recognized our need to loosen up our approach, and we began to make room for language-specific small groups that could meet at the church.[4] Still, things didn't really come together for us until April 2008, thanks to David Uth, who at the time was the senior pastor of First Baptist Church in Orlando, Florida. I was in Orlando to speak at a conference held annually at the church and had arranged to meet David one morning at the urging of his sister, Linda, a member of Mosaic. As we chatted, David shared a personal story that profoundly affected my approach to multi-ethnic ministry.

David told me that he had grown up in Arkansas, where his father was a Southern Baptist pastor during the civil rights movement. Since David's grandfather had immigrated to the United States from Denmark, David's father was keenly aware of the difficulties nonwhites faced at the time in the segregated states of the American South. Indeed, he believed that the local church was a place that should extend the love of God to all people, and David's father made it clear that African Americans would be welcome in his otherwise all-white congregation. It was then that the proverbial crap hit the fan.

First, the deacons approached David's father and demanded that he revise his views on the subject. When he refused, they turned up the heat. One day, two men from the Ku Klux Klan came to his house to deliver a subtle threat: "We think it's wise for you to go along with the deacons in this matter," they said. "It'd be an awful shame if something was to happen to your lovely family." It was then David's father responded in a way that would forever seal upon his son's heart a commitment to loving all people — regardless of ethnic or economic background.

"Now, fellas," his father said, "I'm a deer hunter. I can drop a deer at three hundred yards with a single shot. Fact is, my yard is not that big."

Clear on what he was suggesting, the two men left, and as it turned out, no harm ever did come to the Uth family. As you might expect, however, David's father soon lost his position in that church and was subsequently blacklisted within his own denomination for the remainder of his ministry. Thankfully, his understanding of God's Word and his commitment to the local church as a place for all people lives on in the heart and ministry of his son. And as a pastor, David is now helping his church to transition from a homogeneous church into a multi-ethnic one.

To illustrate his approach, David drew a chart for me, a figure I have since developed further into a model I call "Graduated Inclusion" (fig. 8).

Graduated inclusion is what we now practice at Mosaic. Notice how the four outer circles, which represent different 1.0 groups, are overlapped by the inner circle and square? This allows for a

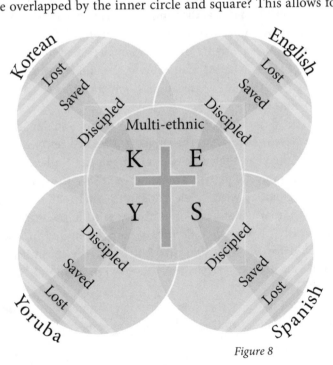

Figure 8

both/and approach to evangelism, discipleship, and leadership development, involving the entire congregation.

The lined outer section of the 1.0 circles represents HUP-driven outreach that targets various ethnic groups for the purpose of evangelism. This includes evangelistically focused worship services, ESL (English as a second language) classes, and other programs or events done in a style and language most familiar to first-generation internationals.

Again, let me be clear: there are only two reasons why we have determined to provide such cross-cultural ministry as described in the lined outer section of the diagram. First, for the purpose of evangelism — to preach and share the gospel in a way that is most accessible to the 1.0s we are trying to reach. Second, to establish an initial level of comfort for internationals coming into the church who are not yet fluent in the language or culture of the United States. For all involved, then, we make it clear that we have no intention of creating an ethnic-specific church. Instead we have adopted the HUP as *an evangelistic tool* for ethnic-specific outreach and as part of a more comprehensive strategy for building *one* healthy multi-ethnic church.

Notice next the somewhat triangular zones that exist at the point where the 1.0 circles intersect the square of the multi-ethnic congregation. This area represents the reality that some 1.0s who embrace Christ as Savior will still need initial discipleship in forms and languages they understand. Once again, we gladly provide these opportunities to those who are perhaps still reluctant to engage or are wary of the larger body, and as a way of helping them grow more comfortable at Mosaic over time.

Finally, the circle inside the square that overlaps all the other circles represents 1.0s and English-speakers alike who are involved with the greater body of Mosaic, integrated and interacting with one another beyond their own people group. In our case, this includes 1.0s who choose to attend a service that is simultaneously translated over headsets or who are actively serving in the church nursery, in children's or student ministries, with the worship team as a singer or musician, or in some other area of leadership, even though their English may still be limited. In fact, for several years two Latina women — Loli Roeglin and Martha Renteria — have been responsible for setting up the communion table and elements for the entire church two times each month. Another Latino couple, Alex and Sandra Garduno, lead a "Discovering Mosaic" class for 1.0 Hispanics and Latinos who want to get more involved in the church. In fact, increasing numbers of 1.0s now attend integrated LifeGroups at Mosaic. And moving ever closer to the center of the church, into areas of greater influence and responsibility, there are 1.0 Hispanics and Latinos who serve as members of Mosaic's staff and even on our governing board of elders. Figure 9 simply provides another way of looking at this model.

Now, I recognize that the ultimate goal of a church is not merely to produce individuals who can govern the church respon-

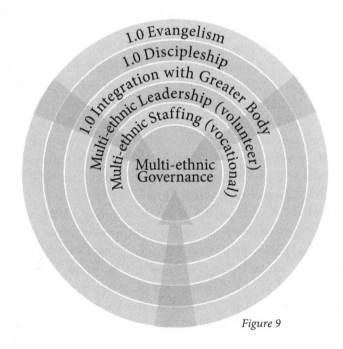

Figure 9

sibly. Nevertheless, we have found that the path of graduated inclusion provides an effective, progressive strategy for seeing 1.0s evangelized, equipped, and established in Christ, individuals who are then able to articulate and replicate the vision of Mosaic to the greater glory of God.

MERGING CHURCHES

Some people have asked, "In what other ways might we pursue increasing diversity in our congregations in the coming years?"

In an online article published in July 2008 by Leadership Network, Dr. Warren Bird, a coauthor of the book *The Multi-Site Church Revolution* (Grand Rapids, Mich.: Zondervan/Leadership Network, 2006), addressed the question, What have you learned about launching an ethnic or multicultural site?[5] Specifically, he compared multi-ethnic churches with multi-ethnic *campuses* of multisite churches. Here's what he had to say: "My prediction is that the increasing diversification of local churches will, in part, be developed through [church] mergers. For instance, our multi-site survey asked, 'Have you used your multi-site approach to assist (or take responsibility for) a declining church?' Of 197 churches that replied to this question, 30 percent said yes, plus 10 percent more said, 'No, but we plan to in the future.' I think those mergers will open the way to more multi-ethnic congregations."

While the concept of a church merger is nothing new, I tend to agree with Warren: enfolding a 1.0 congregation into a more established multi-ethnic church, or a church that genuinely desires to become more diverse in the future, is a viable way to expedite the blending of ethnicities in a single congregation. Yes, such a merger, when rightly conceived and executed, will be beneficial to both churches. On the one hand, homogeneous churches that are pursuing the multi-ethnic vision will immediately benefit from the addition of diverse staff and people to the mix, and the merger provides a visible sign of their commitment to transformation. On the other hand, the 1.0 congregation will often benefit from the additional ministries provided, including a children's or student ministry more in line with the integrated schools their kids are likely attending.

At Mosaic, we recently experienced the fruit of such a merger when we joined with an existing Hispanic and Latino congregation in August 2008. On that day, we formally enfolded that congregation into the larger body of Mosaic, and approximately one hundred Hispanics and Latinos (including two full-time pastors) — formerly the people of Iglesia Nazareno del Samaritano — committed to walk, work, and worship God together with us as part of one church body. And the merger has proven to be quite a blessing for all. By enfolding this congregation, for example, we were able to redirect the money they were paying each month in rent and utilities toward paying their two Latino pastors, whose compensation, due to the overhead of the building, had been lacking. In addition, their members benefited from our larger facility, our organizational infrastructure, and increased validation that came with the merger. For our part, adding a third service with music and preaching in Spanish instantly increased our presence and credibility among the 1.0 Hispanics and Latinos living in our community. And through graduated inclusion, we have seen firsthand how a more balanced diet of service options can lead to increased understanding, relational development, cross-cultural competency, and partnership within the church for the sake of the gospel.

As with any merger, there are steps of faith that must be taken by everyone involved. Should you pursue such a merger, it is essential that you take the time to build authentic relationships of transparency and trust between the key leaders of each congregation and together begin to pursue a measure of cross-cultural competence prior to your formal enjoinment. Solid relationships of trust and open communication between leaders on the front end will greatly reduce the risk of your merger failing down the road. In addition, churches pursuing this path should commit to their agreements in writing to avoid any miscommunication or confusion about future intentions and plans. For example, prior to our merger with the people of Iglesia Nazareno del Samaritano, we discussed, wrote, and printed an agreement for distribution to the entire congregation on the day of the formal merger. In part, it read,

WHAT IT IS

1. It is an official merger between Iglesia Nazareno del Samaritano and the Mosaic Church of Central Arkansas whereby from now on we will all be known as the Mosaic Church of Central Arkansas.
2. It is an opportunity for expanded, more effective evangelism of first-generation Latinos via Mosaic.
3. It is an opportunity for expanded, more effective discipleship of Latino young people, i.e., second- and third-generation Latinos, via Mosaic.

WHAT IT'S NOT

1. It is (we are) not two churches under one roof. We are one church, now with multiple service options.
2. It does not in any way change our DNA. Rather, it eliminates a barrier we unintentionally established through the years, namely, one that made it difficult for many first-generation Latinos to find Christ and/or a church home with us at Mosaic.
3. It is not an exclusive or intentional segregation of people by ethnic heritage or language, etc. Anyone and everyone is welcome to attend any of Mosaic's worship services or program options!

Having considered these things, you may be interested in the possibility of a merger with another congregation whose people are ethnically or economically different from those currently in your church, but you may be wondering where to get started. Let me suggest a few ideas.

For churches with denominational ties, I recommend you begin by networking with ethnic pastors within your own denomination who share an interest in multi-ethnic ministry. Be aware, however, that you will likely face some opposition to your ideas from denominational leaders who are still committed to the HUP as a model for church growth. Nevertheless, begin by introducing yourself and find ways to develop these relationships, always keeping an eye out for a man or woman of peace whose heart is inclined to your vision for a multi-ethnic church. Regardless of your denominational affiliation, you should also make efforts to introduce yourself to ethnic pastors living close to your church, if for no other reason than to establish cross-cultural friendship and mutual respect. Call to schedule an appointment and introduce yourself to the pastor, share your heart for ministry, and (if he or she is willing) begin a dialogue. As simple as it may sound, this is the very thing I did several years ago when one day I walked into a local Korean church, where the pastor warmly received me. In time, we were discussing a potential merger and were moving toward that possibility. Sadly, he later accepted a new position within his denomination and moved to California, but I remain encouraged by the two years of our friendship. In any event, you will be looking for others who share your theological and philosophical views concerning the church. After the merger is achieved, you will want to honor and respectfully accommodate the 1.0 leadership you bring on to partner with you, working hard to avoid any appearance of condescension.

For example, the founding pastor of Iglesia Nazareno del Samaritano, Osmani Silva, who was the newest member of our staff, came to me shortly after the merger to let me know about a Latino evangelist who would soon be visiting Little Rock. This man, Osmani said, travels throughout the United States and Central and South America, sharing his verifiable testimony of having been shot, declared dead, and then raised to life again by the power of Christ. His story had been documented at the time in a San Salvadorian paper, and we were able to read all about it online. Consequently, Osmani asked if this man could preach at Mosaic. I realized that if not for the merger, Osmani would have probably had the evangelist preach in his church, so I honored his request and allowed the man to speak at Mosaic. We introduced him in our Sunday morning services and invited people to hear his testimony later that evening. I felt it was important to show respect for Osmani in this way, letting him know that he would have influence in his new church.

In another instance, Osmani came to me with a request that we support a member of their (now our) congregation, a lay minister who had been in Mexico for three months ministering in three churches Iglesia Nazareno del Samaritano had planted. So I asked Osmani, "How much would your church have given him?" And he said, "Oh, I don't know, we might have taken an offering; maybe fifty to one hundred dollars." Instead of agreeing to that amount, I suggested that we give him three hundred dollars, one hundred dollars for every month he had been gone ministering. In this way too we accommodated Osmani and sought to validate the merger. Making decisions in this manner has gone a long way toward building initial trust and respect among everyone involved. I'll never forget the time when Jorge Bazan, a Latino worship leader who also came to Mosaic with Osmani in the merger, told us in a staff meeting, "In a church where we used to meet, they told us we were welcome. But they made sure to lock the doors of every room in that place before we arrived to worship on Sunday afternoons. But here at Mosaic, every door is open to us!" While to me it seemed like such a small detail, it was quite apparent that for Jorge and the people of Iglesia Nazareno del Samaritano, this was an empowering act of respect and trust.

UNDOCUMENTED INVOLVEMENT

Another philosophical question that those who lead a multiethnic church will undoubtedly ask is, What are we to do with undocumented immigrants? You will wonder how best to meet their needs and concerns and, more specifically, what are the ways in which they can be involved in the church. Let me share some insights based on my experience at Mosaic.

First, remember that God is concerned with people, not borders, and when it comes to serving the spiritual, material, and physical needs of immigrants, there is strong biblical precedent for getting involved. Indeed, the Old Testament records the specific commands that God gave to the nation of Israel on this matter when he spoke to Moses:

> "Do not mistreat an alien or oppress him, for you were aliens in Egypt.... Do not oppress an alien; you yourselves know how it feels to be aliens, because you were aliens in Egypt" (Ex. 22:21; 23:9).

> "When an alien lives with you in your land, do not mistreat him. The alien living with you must be treated as one of your native-born. Love him as yourself, for you were aliens in Egypt. I am the LORD your God" (Lev. 19:33 – 34).

> "Cursed is the man who withholds justice from the alien, the fatherless or the widow" (Deut. 27:19).

Still, quoting verses like this does not mean that this is all the Bible has to say on the subject.

In addition, New Testament teaching makes it clear that as followers of Christ, we are to honor the law and respect the rulers of our land. Luke, in his gospel, records the teaching of Jesus in this regard: "[Jesus] saw through their duplicity and said to them, 'Show me a denarius. Whose portrait and inscription are on it?' 'Caesar's,' they replied. He said to them, 'Then give to Caesar what is Caesar's, and to God what is God's'" (Luke 20:23 – 25).

Elsewhere, in a letter to the churches, Peter writes, "Submit yourselves for the Lord's sake to every authority instituted among men: whether to the king, as the supreme authority, or to governors, who are sent by him to punish those who do wrong and to commend those who do right" (1 Peter 2:13 – 14).

How, then, should the church respond to undocumented immigrants living in their midst? How should we resolve the apparent tension of the Scriptures in this matter?

In the earliest days of our church, one of our members was issued a traffic ticket. Later we learned that he was undocumented. A year or so after this incident, he received a second citation from local police, who discovered that he had received his driver's license fraudulently by using a fake Social Security number. Though he was a very hard worker and in every other way a law-abiding member of the community, this individual soon received a letter from the United States Bureau of Citizenship and Immigration, requiring him to leave the country within thirty days. He chose to ignore the letter and remain in Little Rock.

Out of concern for him and what his decision might mean for the church, I met with local immigration officials to discuss his situation. Among other things, I learned that a church is not required by law to know or to determine the legal status of its members. The officials explained to me that a church's leaders do not in any way violate the laws of the land when they minister to or involve undocumented immigrants in their church while conducting normal, expected operations related to ministry. Having heard from several people that it was illegal to transport undocumented immigrants, I asked them what they thought about sending a bus into neighborhoods to pick up people who were in need of a ride to church on Sunday mornings. In response, they clarified for me that the law addresses "aiding and abetting": that is, knowingly transporting or harboring undocumented immigrants in return for profit or for other clandestine reasons. In other words, there is nothing wrong with providing rides to and from church or benevolently assisting undocumented immigrants in similar ways.

I still remember them sharing with me, as I left their offices, how understaffed they were and how they were not terribly concerned with deporting hardworking, otherwise law-abiding individuals (such as our church member). They were more interested in catching undocumented immigrants who are in this country committing crimes, and also U.S. citizens who are taking advantage of them illegally. "Don't worry," they said, "we will not be raiding your church anytime soon!"

Since that meeting, our leadership has come to understand that we are in no way restricted by law from interacting with undocumented immigrants or empowering them to serve in any capacity at Mosaic. However, because our elder board must conduct legal business from time to time on behalf of the church, we have decided not to appoint an undocumented immigrant to serve as an elder. In addition, we do not knowingly (nor can a church legally) hire an undocumented immigrant. This is important to note, as increasingly employers, including churches, are responsible for validating paperwork in this regard. Many times we have been heartbroken as we have turned away otherwise likeable and qualified candidates. I wish there were a simple solution to this problem or that we could somehow wave a magic wand and fix the whole undocumented situation (both for the church and for the country). But this, unfortunately, is the reality of our times. We continue to pray for a solution to this difficult problem.

MISSIONAL? IT'S WHO WE ARE

Have you ever wondered why it was the church at Antioch and *not* the church at Jerusalem that sent the first missionaries into the world? God said go (Matt. 28:19 – 20; Acts 1:8), but the saints in Jerusalem said no! In fact, it wasn't until the church at Jerusalem was persecuted that individuals were forced to carry the message of Christ to other lands and people (Acts 11:19 – 20). In contrast, the church at Antioch was proactive and eager to send Paul and Barnabas forth to distant lands. But why?

For all the talk about being "missional" today, much of the conversation has grown out of a white, homogeneous context. To be clear, I am very thankful for church leaders who are challenging people to look beyond themselves to meet the needs of hurting people, challenging believers to *go and be the church* in homes and neighborhoods, cafés, bars, and clubs, in the workplace, the work-

PURSUING THE DREAM

Ed Lee, Lead Pastor
Mosaic Community Covenant Church, Sugar Land, Texas

Those of us who are engaged in multi-ethnic ministry are motivated by a strong and clear commitment to preaching of the gospel so that many will come to faith and trust in Jesus Christ. Yet there are subtle differences in our approaches to developing healthy and effective multi-ethnic churches.

Some, seeing the changing demographics of their community, are considering how to better prepare or position their church to be more effective in reaching out to their unsaved neighbors. For example, they may offer simultaneous Spanish translation of their Sunday morning message, hoping to reach those more comfortable worshiping in Spanish. Some multi-ethnic churches employ various cultural elements in their approaches, attempting to be both inclusive and missional, while reminding members of the Great Commission and emphasizing the importance of returning to countries of origin on short-term mission trips to advance God's kingdom. Still others, convicted by the sin of prejudice still present in society and in the church, seek to develop an approach that emphasizes healthy race relations in order to demonstrate the power of God's love with credibility through the tearing down of walls that continue to separate and divide the people of God. This is the approach we take at Mosaic Community Covenant Church (MCCC).

Of course, there are barriers in any approach that must be overcome. For instance, there may be a "this is our church" attitude among entrenched church members, where they find it difficult to accept or include those who are different from them. Other people may encounter challenging barriers as they try connecting with someone from a different culture, especially if cultural practices and mindsets seem too foreign. For us at MCCC, the barrier may be that we fear going deeper in understanding the pain of prejudice and racism that has caused so much suffering; we might fear looking back and surfacing some ugly emotions and painful experiences from the past without knowing or realizing the impact such things have on our effectiveness today in relating to others of a different race. On the other hand, we might fear being blamed for our past, or what some might term as "white bashing." The fact is, we are in uncharted waters, longing for a clear and safe passage to our destination—healthy race relations—or, as more biblically defined, being one in Christ.

We are a church that longs to see the fulfillment of our Lord's last prayer (John 17), the perfection of unity and oneness, lived out in our midst. That's what keeps us going. We have a desire to go deeper in our understanding of one another and want to share history
cont.

together, no matter how painful it can be at times. That's what keeps us growing. We are learning to apologize for the pains and injustices that members of our race or ethnicity have inflicted in the past. That's what helps us become one. And we are experiencing true forgiveness, acceptance, and love—that's what keeps us moving forward, even when it's only a few inches at a time. In the end, we want to be effective witnesses for God and living testimonies of the power of his love, demolishing strongholds and tearing down the walls that divide us and keep us from being truly united as one in Christ. Believing this can happen in our church is what keeps us pursuing the dream.

out center, and on the college campus. But if the missional mindset is not a natural outgrowth of the prevailing model of church ministry, perhaps it demonstrates a weakness in our understanding of the church itself.

At Mosaic we have found, much as was probably true in Antioch, that a missional mindset is inherent to the very culture and DNA of a healthy multi-ethnic church. In these congregations, missions is not a program; it is a reflection of the church itself, who we are. Since cross-cultural ministry is an everyday reality in such an environment, missional engagement is therefore central to the life of the multi-ethnic church and the practice of its ministry.

This is why we began to distribute food, clothing, and other material goods to members on a very small scale in 2004. The fact is, our own members were hungry, in need of clothing, beds, refrigerators, and many other things we had no systematic way of providing. In those days, we began our work by simply asking the body to donate as needs arose, and most of the time our people came through. In time and through the leadership of Cesar Ortega, Mosaic's pastor of community engagement, we began to store donated items in order to be more adequately prepared. As word of mouth spread within the community, the demand on our time and resources grew with each passing year, requiring greater organization, more planning, and the involvement of people beyond our own staff and membership. After assisting some 250 people in the first twelve months of ministry, five years later this ministry — the Orchard — now serves more than ten thousand people a year!

LESSONS LEARNED

In closing, let me make one thing perfectly clear: diversity in the body is not, in and of itself, sufficient to ensure that you will have a healthy, biblical church. Pursuing ethnic blends does not mean that we should fail to promote or practice well-established principles of local church development. As I am writing this book, my publisher (Zondervan) is releasing another work titled *Ten Stupid Things That Keep Churches from Growing*, written by Geoff Surratt, a good friend and fellow pastor.[6] The principles he discusses in his book, while not directly related to multi-ethnic church ministry, are still valid and important principles for any church determined to grow qualitatively and quantitatively, regardless of whether it is pursuing the multi-ethnic vision. Be careful, then, not to throw out the baby with the bathwater while rejecting some, but not all, of the conventional wisdom concerning local church development. This is a lesson we learned the hard way.

Two years into our existence as a church, our elder board was made up of three individuals: myself, Harry Li, and Harold Nash. Since we were growing, we decided to add five men to our board. In choosing these men, our first (and only) step was to study the biblical qualifications of an elder (1 Tim. 3:1 – 9; Titus 1:6 – 9), scan the horizon of current membership, and select from among the body a few who met these standards. At the time, we naively failed to recognize that the biblical standards are given only to help surface potential candidates — they don't necessarily presume their selection. Though our candidates appeared to meet the biblical qualifications, we failed to push deeper to examine each man's abilities, personality, life and ministry experience, and potential fit within the existing team. We simply trusted that good men in good faith with good intentions would all understand just who we were and where we were heading as a church. Little did we realize, however, that our failure to articulate a more detailed vision for the church beyond our multi-ethnic DNA would eventually cause a split in our church leadership. Within three years, three of the five men we had selected decided not only to withdraw from the elder board but also to leave the church.

Their departure was a very painful ordeal for Harry and me, and for our wives as well, to endure. In many ways, the division shook our entire church to the core. On some days it felt to us like the wheels were coming off. At other times I wondered if we would survive or ever again experience thriving, successful ministry. Fortunately, we did not give up but instead sought the counsel of seasoned church planters in our local area, whose encouragement proved to be invaluable in the restoration of our determination and our damaged emotions.

Among other things, we learned that the way forward for our church would involve committing ourselves to a more comprehensive vision, one that would expand our identity beyond the multi-ethnic vision and chart a course for the next five to ten years of our work. In putting this together on paper, we were encouraged to consider the location, size, and function of future facilities we might one day hope to own, to project the size of our staff and congregation within the coming years, to determine future expansion possibilities through campus or church planting, and to define more specifically the role and responsibilities of senior leadership. So together as elders we drafted, revised, and adopted a document, not only to guide us through our present challenges but also as a blueprint for avoiding directional confusion in the future. Since developing this tool, we have greatly reduced the amount of misunderstandings among our leadership team. In addition, we have developed an elders' handbook that contains nearly one hundred pages of useful information and the experiential wisdom of local church leaders from around the country. Today we use these resources to train future leaders within our church.

Though the wisdom other pastors shared with us had not been acquired within the context of a multi-ethnic church, these pastors guided us during this difficult season by passing on timeless truths about local church development, truths they had mined throughout years of ministry, validated by researchers and practitioners alike. We have since learned that many of these principles can be applied in any church situation, even a multi-ethnic one. Had someone thought to apply them in the early days of our ministry, we could have avoided several years of wandering in the dark, making obvious mistakes, and possibly the departure of nearly half of our first elder board! However, in those early days, we were more immediately concerned with setting the multi-ethnic DNA of our church. Looking back, I realize that the narrowness of our vision kept us from appreciating the wisdom of others, and we overlooked some simple truths about local church development that should not be ignored. I trust that in your own passion for building a healthy multi-ethnic church, you will not make the same philosophical mistake.

QUESTIONS FOR REFLECTION AND DISCUSSION

1. Discuss your understanding of the models presented in this chapter. How might the model of graduated inclusion be applied within your own ministry context? What are you currently doing or might you envision doing in the future to move your church away from a mindset that values intended exclusion?

2. What, if anything, are you doing to meet and build relationships with ethnic pastors leading 1.0 churches in your area? What if any value might you see in doing so? As you consider ethnic churches in your area, are there any prospects for pur-

suing a merger at some point in the future for the benefit of everyone involved? If so, what is a next step you might take in that direction?

3. Consider your own views concerning illegal immigration in the United States today. On a more personal level, do you know or suspect anyone in your church to be undocumented? If so, how does this shape your thinking on the subject? If not, how can you imagine it might? Are your thoughts and opinions on the matter informed by Scripture or more by personality, past experience, personal preference, or party politics?

4. Does your church have a well-defined five- to ten-year strategic plan on paper? If so, in what ways does it address the growing diversity of our society and, more specifically, the increasing diversity of the community in which your church is (or will be) established? If not, how might you begin to plan with intentionality and pursue greater diversity in the years to come for the sake of the gospel? Beyond the multi-ethnic vision, in what ways does your strategic plan address more nuts-and-bolts concerns of local church development in your context?

5. What key thought, revelation, or insight will you take away from this chapter? What is God asking you to do in response?

Chapter 5

CAN I POUR YOU A CUP?

Overcoming the Practical Obstacles

Each of you should look not only to your own interests,
but also to the interests of others.

— *Philippians 2:4*

WHO'S TO SAY?

Recently I attended a meeting with leaders from four or five churches in Little Rock, hosted by a local university. We had been invited to consider how future partnerships, in cooperation with the university and local business leaders, might serve to improve literacy and math proficiency among students attending several schools in our area. Since each of the churches in attendance was already involved in one or more of these schools, university officials were hopeful that more synergistic efforts could produce exponential results.

Perhaps it was too much to expect.

As one neutral observer later shared with me, ego and self-interest were painfully evident to some who attended that day, despite the polite discussion. In addition to subtle tensions hidden beneath the surface of our discussion, there were divergent opinions about what we should do and how best to proceed. And I have no doubt that many of the opinions were shaped by race and class distinctions. For instance, some of the white people in the room were partial to pursuing a program governed by a business plan that could be implemented to recruit, train, and deploy volunteers to produce measurable results. On the other hand, some of the black people who attended seemed far more concerned with ensuring that relationships were first established with families and that their own communities were involved in the process.

My experience in this meeting illustrates an important principle: when working together with others who have a different ethnic, economic, or educational background, always remember that *your* way is just *a* way and not *the* way to approach or resolve an issue. Mutually respectful interaction with people who are different from you, at formative stages of ministry development, is one of the first challenges you will face in seeking to build a healthy multi-ethnic church.

For instance, "white" churches interested in leaving their own neighborhoods to serve in more integrated and economically depressed areas of the city would benefit by listening to the people they are trying to serve and by seeking to incorporate the ideas of those who live and work in the community into their own. Failing to involve community leaders in the decision-making process will, in all likelihood, lead to yet another frustrated effort to engage urban complexities with a suburban mindset. That's not to say that urban church leaders always have the answers. It's just a reminder that mutual respect must be established and maintained, apart from any personal or corporate agendas, when we engage together in ministry across demographic lines.

Having served in a segregated, suburban megachurch prior to planting Mosaic, I'm quite familiar with a businesslike approach to church ministry, both its blessings and its pitfalls. To establish the credibility of Mosaic, however, I had to learn and apply the very principles I'm suggesting in order to meet the *immediate* needs of diverse people coming through our doors.

The fact is, there are many different ways for you to practically pursue multi-ethnic ministry, and there are many different ways to help your church grow and develop. It's not important, then, to follow a precise model; allow yourself the freedom to dream, experiment, fail, revise your dreams, and try again. Most important, continue making an effort to trust those who have different ideas than you do during this process, something I was forced to do with Cesar Ortega, one of our elders and Mosaic's pastor of community engagement, when he first suggested the idea of distributing food and clothing to meet the immediate needs of our people. Had I thought too long about it on the front end and based a decision to move forward with his suggestion on my own limited experience with such programs, we might never have begun the ministry or seen it develop into the amazing blessing it has become today to so many in our community.

For the remainder of this chapter, let's explore some of the other practical challenges that you can expect to face as you engage in multi-ethnic local church ministry, and as we do, I'll provide suggestions for overcoming the obstacles.

FROM HOMOGENEOUS TO MULTI-ETHNIC

Given my passion for the multi-ethnic church, I am often asked whether I believe that monoracial (white or black) or mono-ethnic (Mexican, Korean, or other) churches are somehow unbiblical or functioning outside the will of God. So let me be clear about this: I do not believe such churches are unbiblical. However, I do believe that local churches are biblically mandated to respond in some way to the prayer of Christ in John 17:20 – 23.

As we have already discussed, Jesus envisioned his church as multi-ethnic, praying, "I in them and You in Me, that they may be *perfected in unity*, so that the world may know that You sent Me, and loved them, even as You have loved Me" (John 17:23 NASB, emphasis mine).

In the language of the New Testament, the English word *perfected* is translated from the Greek root *teleiow*, meaning "to carry through completely, to accomplish, finish, bring to an end" or "to add what is yet wanting in order to render a thing full."[1] In other words, the implication is that unity — like the process of sanctification in a believer's life — is not something achieved all at once but something progressively rendered over time in a people willing to pursue the heart of God.

Building a healthy multi-ethnic church, then, requires a great deal of prayer, patience, and persistence over time. In fact, if you are leading a homogeneous congregation in need of transformation, the last thing you will want to do is split the church in the name of unity! Yet this is exactly what will happen if you move too quickly in your pursuit of this biblical vision.

With this in mind, figure 10 presents a continuum leading from absolute ethnic homogeneity to the unity and diversity of heaven. So where is your church currently located on this continuum? In addition, ask yourself the questions, What should we do practically to make this vision a reality? and, How and when can we do things realistically? In fact, take some time now to consider the next logical step or two your church might take to press on toward maturity in the matter. Keep in mind that the goal is not to precisely locate where you are on the continuum. Simply use it as a guide for envisioning the future of your church, for giving your leaders a sense of where you hope one day to be, and even for establishing a commitment to making that happen.[2] In the end, actions will speak louder than words!

Sociologist colleagues who promote the vision of the multi-ethnic church have established a numeric value — the 20 percent threshold — as a way of identifying a church as multiracial. According to them, a church is considered multiracial (I use the term *multi-ethnic*) if no single ethnic group makes up more than 80 percent of the congregation.[3] However, the vast majority of multi-ethnic church practitioners today not only feel that this bar is too low but also recognize that there is much more that defines an authentic multi-ethnic church than merely counting heads on any given Sunday morning. While it is true that sociological research shows that societies and institutions must make systemic adjustments when the racial composition of their population reaches 20 percent or more, still such numbers provide just one measurement to help you determine where you are along the continuum we have just discussed. Additional factors you must take into account include the diverse composition of your leadership, the broad acceptance within your church of various styles of worship, and the cross-cultural transferability of forms and practices of ministry within your congregation. All of these further define the reality and credibility of a church that describes itself as multi-ethnic. Practically speaking, pastors should be careful not to rely upon numbers alone in declaring their churches multi-ethnic. Still, numerical percentages give us one way of defining or describing success. In fact, I am excited to promote through my writing and speaking the very realistic goal of achieving 20 percent diversity in 20 percent of churches throughout the United States by the year 2020. And I hope that by the year 2050, 50 percent of our churches will have achieved 50 percent diversity — again, all for the sake of the gospel.

The Perfection of Unity: A Corporate Reflection*

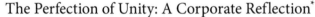
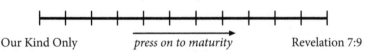

Our Kind Only   *press on to maturity*   Revelation 7:9

1. Ask, Where is our church on the continuum?
    a. What do we understand theologically?
    b. What do we believe philosophically?
2. Ask, What is the next logical step or two our church can take to move forward in pursuit of ethnic blends?
    a. What should we do practically?
    b. How and when can we do it realistically?

* For examples of various stages on the continuum, see Building a Healthy Multi-ethnic Church, *180 – 81.*

Figure 10

VARIABLE BLENDS

According to my good friend Ed Lee, lead pastor of Mosaic Community Covenant Church in Sugar Land, Texas, not all multi-ethnic churches are alike. Through his own experience and interaction within the movement, he has noticed that subtle differences in approach and strategy give multi-ethnic churches their own practical look and feel. With this in mind, Ed has identified at least five major variations on the multi-ethnic church, and I'll share them here with you. As you read this section and study the corresponding chart (appendix 4), note that the lines of distinction between such churches are often blurred and, therefore, that churches are not as neatly classified as some would hope. In other words, a given church may exhibit any number of the traits or tendencies Ed describes. Nevertheless, I believe that a brief consideration of Ed's findings can bring greater clarity to your vision and more purpose to your pursuit of ethnic blends.

Multi-ethnic Church 1: An Emphasis on First-generation (1.0) Outreach

The first variation on the multi-ethnic church places a distinct emphasis on local outreach. These multi-ethnic churches are committed to empowering diverse leadership, with the goal of reaching a particular racial/ethnic group that is often nearby. Motivated to fulfill the Great Commission, this multi-ethnic church may provide space for ethnocentric worship, lend financial support in hiring staff, or even establish a separate-language venue under its own governance. As a concern, this model risks mono-ethnic separation by establishing an us-and-them status quo.

Multi-ethnic Church 2: An Emphasis on World Missions

The second variation Ed has identified places an emphasis on world missions. These multi-ethnic churches are committed to mobilizing an ethnically diverse membership to help them connect with and return to (with other members of the church) their countries of origin for the purpose of short- and long-term evangelistic impact or church planting. Flags hung from the church's ceiling, or a strategically placed world map, will often reflect the various countries from which members have come or to which the church has sent missionary teams; this helps to keep the mission emphasis in view. As a concern, these churches are sometimes too globally focused and may potentially neglect to reach out to meet the needs of their own community or of homeless individuals living right outside their doors.

Multi-ethnic Church 3: An Emphasis on Local Evangelism

The third variation places an emphasis on local evangelism. These multi-ethnic churches are committed to the intentional pursuit of cross-cultural competence in an increasingly diverse society. They value accommodation over assimilation and encourage diverse cultural expressions of faith throughout the body, from the pulpit to the nursery and at every station in between. Multiple teaching pastors of various ethnicities, and worship leaders incorporating a variety of styles, all rotating from week to week, model shared responsibility and appreciation for the multi-ethnic nature of the church — one which, in all likelihood, simultaneously translates its message into one or more languages. As a concern, these churches may be too idealistic in expecting people to embrace the vision without regard for their own personal comforts.

Multi-ethnic Church 4: An Emphasis on Racial Reconciliation

The fourth variation places an emphasis on racial reconciliation. These multi-ethnic churches intentionally address the pain of injustice, prejudice, and racism that hinders people from developing deeper, more meaningful relationships with one another. They believe that this pain has contributed to the segregation of the local church and undermined the very credibility of our message of God's love for all people. Because of this, these churches seek to manifest the reality and power of God's love by breaking down dividing walls. Church leadership emphasizes oneness rather than diversity, and instead of celebrating diverse cultures, the church strives to create one new culture — a culture of acceptance in which people are willing to work through the lingering effects of systemic racism. As a concern, these churches may be unrealistic in expecting to fully solve the problems of prejudice that yet linger in society without addressing the spiritual transformation of the human heart.

Multi-ethnic Church 5: An Emphasis on Community Engagement

The fifth variation places an emphasis on community engagement. These multi-ethnic churches develop cross-cultural relationships within the urban context, in an effort to reach various subcultures in relevant ways. They value creativity and innovation in extending the love of God to diverse peoples who are attracted through nontraditional forms of communication, artistic expression, or real-world environments such as a bar or club. Generally, these churches attract a younger audience as they live out and promote an incarnational approach to ministry within the cultures they are trying to reach. As a concern, these churches may be too self-serving, and thus the multi-ethnic nature of the work may be more a by-product than an intended outcome of the ministry.

WHAT ABOUT MUSIC?

Another practical question I am often asked to address involves the worship service and, more specifically, how to incorporate various musical genres in order to accommodate the diverse preferences of people attending. Before speaking to these considerations, however, I suggest first and foremost that leaders address attitudes within their congregation. Below, then, are three common responses I return to time and time again in helping diverse people gain a more holistic perspective of who we are and to whom we are responsible. Each is rhetorical in nature, with a bit of sarcasm thrown in to further make the point.

1. "Where in the Bible does it say it's about what you want or what you like?"
2. "I thought we are supposed to align the church with Christ's agenda, not to align the church with our own."[4]
3. "Church shopping? You mean, looking for the best deals and what's in it for me?"

Of course, I do not mean to be flippant or disrespectful in speaking to anyone along these lines. Yet it is important to adjust attitudes from time to time or to remind the church to whom it answers and belongs — namely, Jesus Christ.

Once attitudes are aligned (Phil. 2:4), there are many other ways in which we can go on to address the challenge of corporate worship. Through the years at Mosaic, however, we have followed one of these three basic approaches:

1. *Blended sets.* This first approach seeks to incorporate a variety of musical genres within one service. And when done with excellence, this approach provides a wonderful reflection of the people and passion of churches such as Mosaic. Unfortunately, we have found it takes a great deal of time, talent, and tweaking to produce a diverse pallet of sound and song without disrupting the flow of worship or appearing too agenda driven. Blended worship sets can sometimes seem choppy and contrived if you do not have time and talent to pull it off naturally. Typically, we employ this first option only for our bigger services such as those during the Easter or Christmas seasons.

2. *Weekly rotations.* This next approach relies upon the development of several different stylistic variations and upon worship leaders willing to rotate throughout each month on a weekly basis. For example, on the first Sunday of the month, we might provide a gospel music set, followed the next week by a more guitar-driven sound. On the third week, a choir might sing, while on the fourth week, songs might be sung in Spanish and the music played with a Latin feel. In addition, it can be both fun and refreshing to mix singers and musicians in such a way that they expand their own understanding of worship, and they will often appreciate the opportunity to try something new. At Mosaic, our choir does sing on the third Sunday of every month. However, the rest of the weeks are largely determined by who is or is not available to lead, play, and sing on any given Sunday morning.

3. *Major-minor mornings.* This third approach is the one we typically employ at Mosaic from week to week, and in one sense it offers the best of both worlds. Assuming that we have room for five songs in the service, three or four of them will be led by one worship leader and come from the musical genre that best matches his or her strengths and passions. At another point in the service, we will incorporate a second person leading out in an entirely different style. More often than not, the two leaders will be different ethnically, providing visitors a better sense of the vision and values that inform the church. In this way, we maintain a natural sense of flow and a spirit of authenticity in our music, while still promoting a spirit of inclusion before the congregation.

Of course, the worship service is much more than just the music we sing. We also incorporate diversity within our preaching team and in the other elements of the service. For example, if Steven Weathers (an African American and one of our campus/

ECLECTIC WORSHIP

Daniel Backens, Senior Pastor
New Life Providence Church, Virginia Beach, Virginia

I have found that people of every culture are deeply passionate about their music. In order to build a successful multi-ethnic church, it is vital therefore to create a worship experience that everyone finds meaningful.

The operative word for worship in a multi-ethnic church, I believe, is *eclectic*. In order for a worship set to be strategic, it should take into consideration the different worship styles, traditions, and experiences of your target congregation. In our church, each month we try to sing an even distribution of traditional hymns, contemporary Christian music, gospel music, and urban praise. Of course, doing this with excellence is easier with talented musicians and a motivated congregation, but I believe every church can do something.

I receive more comments about the music in our church—both positive and negative—than about any other single aspect of our ministry. Nothing gives me more of a sinking feeling in the pit of my stomach than when someone says something like, "We sing too much of *their* music" or "The music in this church is too white [or black]." And then there is the occasional really religious comment like, "*Those* folks' music is too emotional and not spiritual enough." Ugh! But I do get some very encouraging feedback as well, such as, "I never want to go back to singing only one kind of worship style. I really feel God's presence in the diversity."

One of the keys to creating an eclectic sound in worship is to continually enforce the value of wholehearted worship rather than emphasizing a particular worship style. I try to consistently teach that the heart is what the Lord is after in worship; he does not favor one genre over another. It is certainly okay to prefer one style to another, but it is not acceptable to believe that one style is better than another.

As a pastor, I try to anticipate objections and fears by also explaining the difference between worship preferences versus biblical convictions, as well as by sharing my own journey. As a hymn-singing Lutheran from the Midwest, I can identify with the challenge of singing something unfamiliar. I encourage everyone to enjoy and participate in new styles of worship rather than be judgmental or passive. It can be fun if you make it fun!

On several occasions, an African American family has walked into our Sunday service for the first time and commented on their feeling of connectivity because they heard a familiar gospel song. I have had similar feedback from Hispanic families who felt included when a chorus was sung in Spanish. Over the years, many have shared with me that they formed their opinion about our church before

cont.

the Sunday service officially started, by simply listening to the preservice music! There is much to learn from their comments.

Through the years, I have discovered that gospel music, the type predominantly sung in African American churches throughout the United States, is driven from a keyboard or organ, whereas the music that some have described as contemporary Christian is most often led from the guitar and has a light rock feel. And by the way, there is a big difference between Southern gospel and gospel music categories! The kind of gospel music I am referring to, then, is also supported generally by a choir that sings in three-part harmony, claps on the offbeat, and moves to the music. Nongospel choruses are most often sung in rhythm on the downbeat and have harmony that is four-part. It is interesting that even the same hymns are often interpreted differently by various cultures!

Years ago I heard a phrase that has helped me a lot: "You attract who you are, not who you want." And this is certainly true when it comes to worship music. The greater effort any church makes in creating a worship experience that is dynamic, anointed, and eclectic, the greater the success it will have in becoming authentically multi-ethnic.

teaching pastors) is preaching on a given Sunday, Harry Li (who is Asian American) might lead communion, and I (who am white) will do the announcements. You get the picture.

BEYOND THE MUSIC

Concerning the worship service, we also recognize or celebrate (when appropriate) a variety of ethnic-specific holidays on Sunday mornings throughout the calendar year, whether they are civic in nature or more specifically rooted in one culture or another. For instance, in 2009 Mosaic observed Black History Month and on one particular Sunday replayed a popular video of world-renowned recording artist Wintley Phipps, an African American. On the video, Phipps tells the story and origin of the song "Amazing Grace" and of its composer, John Newton. Before becoming a Christian, Newton was the captain of a slave ship. According to Phipps, many believe that he penned the words to "Amazing Grace" as he listened to the sorrowful chants emanating from the belly of his ship — the tune being sung (or moaned) by the slaves he was transporting around the world. In the video, Phipps points out that in most hymnals, "Amazing Grace" is attributed to "unknown" (symbolic of so many who lost their identities in the scourge of slavery) and that, ironically, the song can be played by using only the black keys on a piano. According to author Rick Payne, these notes represent the pentatonic scale that "is not unique to western musical tradition. Similar scales exist in parts of Africa, and it is fair to assume they would have arrived with the slaves well before the birth of the blues. These pentatonic notes were somehow stressed [over time] into what we call blue notes [today]."[5]

Learning the powerful history behind this popular song, and the tenor (no pun intended) in which the song is delivered on the video, cut to the heart of all those in attendance that day. Therefore, when you are considering ethnic-specific holidays, don't be afraid to incorporate elements like these into Sunday worship. Sure, you may be accused of pandering to the politically correct cause, but since every nation, tribe, people, and language will be represented before the throne one day — and, I might add, worshiping God with one voice (Rev. 7:9 – 10) — remind your critics that it doesn't hurt to begin getting to know about one another and together start singing his praises now!

One final note (okay, pun intended) here. Translating all of your worship resources into one or more languages requires a good bit of administration and attention to detail, and the task can be overwhelming. In our case, every sermon slide, every lyric projected on the screens, and every bulletin or handout has to be translated into Spanish. Why? For one reason: it provides a living illustration of what the apostle Paul teaches us in 1 Corinthians 9:19 – 23. By providing translation services, we who speak English become servants to our Hispanic neighbors so that we might win them all the more! Through the years, we have lost count of how many Central and South American brothers and sisters have been won to Christ through the ministry of Mosaic, but I believe it has been a significant number. And our Latino/Hispanic community appreciates these gestures, both our respect for and commitment to their culture.

In the end, don't be afraid to ask questions that will help you learn what helps or hinders diverse people in their worship. Read books to educate yourself so that you can better understand another's cultural perspective. And, most important, have fun in the process!

WHAT ABOUT STAFFING?

Let me encourage you to empower diverse leaders, sooner than later, by applying this core commitment through volunteers. Indeed, diversifying your leadership team does not require additional funds or resources. Even in the best of financial times, we should not be too quick to hire before considering individuals who are gifted to serve and willing to lead responsibly without receiving compensation. Given the economic diversity so often accompanying a multi-ethnic work, volunteers are not only invaluable; they are essential to fulfilling the vision. At Mosaic, we have diversified our leadership by empowering people like Ronald Young to serve as a lay pastor for new members and Bill Smith as pastor of soul care and stewardship. While Ronald works for a local firm, Bill is the CFO of an online company that provides for his income so he can volunteer his time doing what he loves to do, namely, serve the people of God with his time and talent. In addition, Larry Tarpley, a blind member of our church, volunteers to pastor those with physical disabilities. In fact, if you call our offices, Larry is likely to answer the phone, since he serves as one of two volunteers working the front desk. And Danny Carpenter, a deaf member of our church, has served on his own time to ensure that the sanctuary is cleaned each week prior to Sunday services. None of the people I have mentioned are paid for what they do, yet each is treated as a valued member of our diverse staff team.

Let me also say a word about our elders (Mosaic's governing board). It has taken us quite some time to develop just the right team — one devoted to God, to one another, and to our commitment to diversity. In selecting our elders, we have not rushed into things, nor have we allowed artificial quotas to drive us. As the lead pastor of the church, I was first appointed to serve through the laying on of hands at Antioch Bible Church in Kirkland, Washington, in the summer of 2001. Nine months later I appointed Harold Nash, an African American, to join me in service at the elder level. One year later we added Harry Li, who is an Asian American. Lloyd Hodges (African American) and Bill Head (white) were added in 2004. And in 2009 Cesar Ortega became Mosaic's first elder of Hispanic descent, and Steven Weathers (African American) and Mark Leggett (white) were both added in 2010. For the first time, then, in the nine years since we started, four major ethnicities are currently represented on our governing board.

WHAT ABOUT CHILDREN'S MINISTRY?

As you might expect, there are also practical challenges to building a healthy multi-ethnic children's ministry.[6]

One of the first problems Allen Arnn, Mosaic's associate pastor of ministry development and director of children's ministries, encountered as a new member of our staff had to do with cross-cultural communication and, more specifically, the speed (or lack of it, at times) in which he could produce change. Allen is the type of person who likes to jump in quickly and get things moving. He also happens to be white.

When he was assigned to help develop the children's ministry at Mosaic, he reported to Amos Gray, an African American who oversaw both children's and student ministries at the time. Along with Amos, Allen also worked with one of our very best and most critical volunteer leaders in children's ministries (MoKids), an African American named Karen Walker.

Given his personality, Allen was anxious to get busy to help improve infrastructure and to develop better systems of communication and more effective processes. Looking back, he now realizes that he made a mistake in moving too fast. He was sincerely trying to serve his ministry supervisor and to lead an amazing volunteer under his care. But while mistakes like this are common in every church, there is always added tension in a multi-ethnic church, where people of various backgrounds and life experience are involved together in service. Poor communication in such an environment is a recipe for misunderstanding and distrust. In those early days, one of the most significant lessons Allen would learn was that extra time must be taken to communicate with everyone involved, especially with those who are ethnically different from you.

With this in mind, here are four keys to building trust with others who are serving across the diverse cross-cultural landscape in a multi-ethnic children's ministry.

1. Listen with the sincere goal of understanding, taking the posture of a learner.
2. Do not be afraid to overcommunicate, and do so with great patience and clarity so as to minimize misunderstandings.
3. Spend time getting to know the diverse people you will be involved with, beyond the work at hand.
4. When leading people of various ethnic or economic backgrounds, do not usurp their authority (whether intentionally or unintentionally) if and when they have been given a specific role or responsibility. In brainstorming, be especially careful in making suggestions, for even benign comments, if not carefully stated, can be misinterpreted by others as disrespectful or disempowering.

Though Allen erred in this instance by trying to make changes too quickly, he thinks the opposite error can be just as detrimental: don't allow the fear of offending others to keep you from speaking honestly to them. While it is wise to move slowly, a good leader in a diverse environment should try to navigate the middle ground — taking time to build trust but not becoming paralyzed by the fear of making a personal, racial, or cultural mistake. A good leader must let authentic love and faith work hand in hand in guiding him or her to find a balanced approach when speaking with others.

As Allen continued to talk with Amos and Karen, he was able to work things out over time, to the satisfaction of everyone — and he learned to slow down a bit! Thankfully, his relationships with these individuals grew in strength and effectiveness through the years.

Another obstacle you will likely face in seeking to build a healthy multi-ethnic children's ministry is the lack of good resources, resources that are cross-culturally sensitive and inclusive. The fact is that much of the curricula being developed for children today does not represent the increasing diversity of the North American church, much less that of our culture. This is more than just including appropriate pictures. Many of the teaching examples and illustrations still being used are often slanted toward the dominant culture and, consequently, have to be modified to appeal to the diverse children and workers involved in your ministry.

Another issue is language. While most of the children who attend school in the United States speak English, the parents of more than a few children do not. Therefore, in a multi-ethnic children's ministry, if you want parents and children to interact with the teaching materials at home, you will need to translate take-home resources into the languages spoken by your people. In practice, MoKids' leadership seeks to simplify the English-only resources for parents who are deaf and also translates them into Spanish for parents who cannot read English.

One final warning is to guard against the "at my former church, we did it this way" syndrome. Keep in mind that the way you did things at one church is just *a* way to do things and not necessarily the *best* way to do things in a multi-ethnic environment. For instance, one church may think it a waste of time and money to provide snacks to elementary-school children attending services.

But in all probability, such a church does not have homeless, hungry children attending their services, as we do, for instance, at Mosaic!

WHAT ABOUT STUDENT MINISTRY?

Many of the challenges we face in our ministry to students concern the diversity of the families from which they come.[7] More specifically, we encounter a variety of family perspectives concerning race that can either help or hinder a student's involvement

CREATING THE SWIRL

Chris Williamson, Senior Pastor
Strong Tower Bible Church, Franklin, Tennessee

When trying to identify an authentic multi-ethnic church or ministry, one of the first things I look at is the composition of the leadership. If the leadership team (especially the paid staff) is not ethnically diverse, I immediately begin to question the mission of that particular ministry. In this regard, the old cliché is true: "Actions speak louder than words." By empowering diverse leadership, you'll put your money where your mouth (or mission statement) is.

When people in the pew see those who look like them on the platform, it immediately creates an atmosphere of encouragement and inclusion. Indeed, the proof is in the pudding when there is a distribution of legitimate power and shared responsibility with leaders of other ethnicities. Unfortunately, the leadership in most churches and ministries today is either vanilla or chocolate pudding. It's rare to find a chocolate-and-vanilla swirl!

If multi-ethnic ministry were easy, we'd probably see more diverse representation in local church leadership teams throughout the country. I often hear leaders say they cannot find any viable candidates of other (different) ethnicities to join them in the work. Often, if they actually hire someone and it turns out to be a bust, they are reluctant to try again. I know of a black pastor who once hired a white man to assist him. Things didn't work out, and he had to let the associate go. That black pastor has not hired a white brother since. In another instance, a white friend of mine wanted to plant a multi-ethnic church in a major city and felt it was imperative to have a black man on his team. When my white friend met with me for counsel, I told him that he had the right plan but the wrong black man. Yet he told me that it had been hard enough to find this guy, and he didn't want to delay the start of the work to with our church. For example, a parent once approached our former youth pastor, Amos Gray, to ask if her tenth-grade student would be safe around other students who were involved with Mosaic Student Ministries (MSM). As an African American, Amos recognized that the cross-cultural nature of our ministry had surfaced this parent's unconscious attitudes and fears about people of various ethnic backgrounds. He assured the woman that her child would be fine, and the student went on to have a very positive experience with MSM.

look for someone else. He proceeded on despite my advice, hoping for the best. The experiment eventually blew up, and his current leadership team is all white.

Thankfully, God has blessed our church through the years and has helped us to maintain a decent balance on our staff without it feeling forced or plastic. Recently our pastoral staff became all black when our white pastor stepped out of ministry. Despite an unbalanced representation among the pastors, we remained consistent to our multi-ethnic mission, since the majority of our lay elders were white. In addition, we still had a Hispanic woman, a white woman, and another white male on our staff team as well. Eventually, though, one of our black elders spoke up and reminded us that we needed to diversify our pastoral leadership team, because he felt we were beginning to look like a "black church."

At first I told him that we were fortunate to have black men in pastoral leadership and that I was encouraged to have three when some churches do not even have one. As God would have it, the Holy Spirit moved, and one of our black pastors felt led to plant a diverse church in another city. Immediately, then, we decided as an elder team that we would hire a white man to replace him in the role. We prayed, and soon God provided an amazing white brother to join our pastoral team.

There is a reason why the church at Antioch is the ideal model for multi-ethnic ministry. The diversity of its leadership team says it all (Acts 13:1). As we have learned, you must be intentional, prayerful, patient, and persistent as you pursue competent leaders of various ethnicities to have them join your team. Remember, actions will speak louder than words!

The location of your ministry may also present an obstacle that you will have to overcome in building a healthy multi-ethnic student ministry. Whether you are asking students from the suburbs to come into the city or asking students from the city to venture out into the suburbs, invisible cultural barriers exist that are not easily crossed, especially when you are scheduling evening events. Mosaic is located in an area often described as having the highest rate of violent crime in the entire state. And since approximately 80 percent of our members live outside of the zip code, most of our students are involved in schools or extracurricular activities at locations that aren't close to the church. Those not old enough to drive must rely on their parents or someone else to bring them in, and those with a car are often busy with sports or a job. In situations like this, midweek or other events requiring evening attendance can be adversely affected by the location of your church. Nevertheless, this challenge can be overcome through creative scheduling, by providing rides to and from the church, by establishing discipleship groups that meet in homes or other locations throughout the city, and by enlisting a high-quality, credible volunteer staff that includes committed parents attending your church. Ultimately, we trust in God to build his house, in his way and in his time.

Adding to complexities, and because of our city's history, there have always been places in Little Rock where blacks and whites just will not go at certain times of the night. This makes it difficult for some of our students to invite friends to church. For example, one of our students (black) has been faithfully and frequently asking one of his white friends to attend MSM with him. But his friend always seems to have an excuse for not being able to come. Recently the tables were turned: our student (I'll call him Thad) was asked by his friend to attend a homogeneous megachurch in our city, and Thad went willingly. Later Thad commented that it was just like going to Mosaic, as he found the students in that church to be very friendly and welcoming. So again, the following week, Thad invited his friend to come visit Mosaic. "Truth is, bro'," the boy finally admitted, "my parents have a problem with where Mosaic is located...."

They just have some issues." His statement confirmed again that preexisting attitudes and fears concerning people of other ethnicities run deep in the hearts of some in our city.

Given the diversity of our church, we are forced to think inclusively about every aspect of MSM, from the camps and events we choose to involve our students with to the worship styles and the illustrations we use in teaching. We promote cross-cultural competency and a healthy respect for various cultures by empowering diverse leaders throughout the ministry, from Sunday mornings to Wednesday nights and at other places in between. And through MSM we encourage our students to develop cross-cultural relationships. In these and many other ways, we seek to apply the seven core commitments of a multi-ethnic church to student ministry in order to reach an increasingly diverse generation with the love and hope of Christ.

WHAT SAY YOU?

Like the apostle John describing the life and accomplishments of Jesus in John 21:25, I feel like there is so much more to say about practical matters affecting the development of a healthy multi-ethnic church! Therefore, if you are a multi-ethnic church pastor or leader reading this book and learning valuable lessons through your own experience, I want to encourage you to consider writing, blogging, or in some other way passing your thoughts on to others. In fact, you can do so by going to *www.markdeymaz.com*, where I have created an online forum for discussion related to the chapters of this book. Keep in mind that we are still in the Pioneer Stage of the multi-ethnic church movement, and there is so much more that needs to be learned, developed, and applied. Yes, God is using and teaching you through the experience. Allow him to use you to teach others also.

With this in mind, let's next consider some of the cross-cultural challenges you will surely face in pursuit of ethnic blends.

QUESTIONS FOR REFLECTION AND DISCUSSION

1. Take a moment to:
   A. Review figure 10 and answer the questions within the context of your own church setting. Discuss your observations with your leadership team and/or others in your church. Do others agree with your assessment or suggestions? What does this suggest to you, one way or another?
   B. Review appendix 4. How would you describe your church (as it is or might hope to be) in light of this chart? If you had to identify your church with only one variation on this chart, which one would you pick and why? If you could identify your church with a second variation on this chart, which one would you pick and why?

2. When you consider diversifying the music of your church to promote a spirit of inclusion for others attending, what challenges currently exist or might you anticipate? Of the three basic approaches to music presented in this chapter, which one would best be applied in your context? Is there another approach, not mentioned here, that you can envision or that you believe would better serve your goals and needs in this regard?

3. How diverse is the vocational staff at your church? How diverse are the volunteers who serve throughout the congregation? What specific steps might you take to enlist and empower an increasingly diverse leadership team within the ministry?

4. How prepared are your youth ministries to welcome and serve the needs of minority children and students as well as their families? What color are the dolls in your nursery? What color is Jesus in the picture that hangs on the wall? What specific steps might you take to better promote a spirit of inclusion in the critical area of youth ministries?

5. What key thought, revelation, or insight will you take away from this chapter? What is God asking you to do in response?

Chapter 6

ROASTING FOR FLAVOR

Overcoming the Cross-cultural Obstacles

> I have become all things to all men so that by all possible means I might save some.
>
> — *1 Corinthians 9:22*

UNIQUE BEANS

Unlike Mark, I (Harry) enjoy a good cup of coffee! In fact, at this moment I'm sipping fresh brew at the Java Roasting Café in Little Rock. Here, on occasion, you can catch Roger Williams, Java's chief coffee roaster, at work on the Primo fifty-pound roaster. This massive piece of equipment resembles a rudimentary washing machine merged with a meat grinder on steroids! Nevertheless, it is a highly engineered appliance that precisely controls the temperature of coffee beans throughout the intricate roasting process, a process necessary to achieving the perfect blend.

According to Roger, however, the roasting process is as much art as it is science, and there are no fixed formulas that determine your outcome. First, I'm told, the beans must be heated to achieve an "optimum temperature over a certain amount of time." Once this is done, each bean will crack, releasing the oil contained in its core. Properly roasted, the beans will crack again. This is when most consider the beans to have been brought to a full-flavored roast. Beans roasted beyond the second crack often have a bitter flavor.

So when he roasts beans, Roger must take into account all sorts of variables throughout the process — and that's what the art of roasting is all about. The temperature, the humidity, the number of people coming in and out of the café (because the roasting machine sits next to the door; as it is opened and shut, temperature and humidity inside the café are affected), and, most important, the type of bean being roasted are all important factors he needs to consider. In addition, raw beans that arrive at the store come from the Middle East and beyond, from places in Central and South America such as Costa Rica, Honduras, and Guatemala, from Kenya, India, and other spots around the globe. Each bean, then, is unique, requiring a different mix of variables to achieve its "optimum temperature over a certain amount of time." The result, hopefully, is a well-balanced flavor, unique to that bean. Roasting every bean the same way would all but guarantee coffee that would taste awful — and a coffee shop that would fail.

Similarly, the pursuit of ethnic blends will require you to take multiple variables into account if you are to achieve optimum results. And blending people of different ethnic and economic backgrounds, their personalities and preferences, into a flavorfully attractive community of evangelical faith will likely be as much an art as a science.

The "scientific" side of the work will involve rooting yourself in certain foundational truths such as the centrality and supremacy of Christ (Eph. 2:13 – 18) as well as the message of the gospel. These truths make us one and keep us united, aligned with the Lord, as we seek to follow his will individually and in the church. Our goal is not political correctness but spiritual correctness, for as we have already explained, we are not pursuing unity for the sake of unity; we are pursuing unity for the sake of the gospel! It is important, then, that you provide clear teaching that clarifies foundational truths such as these for a congregation of diverse believers. These truths are infinitely larger than the opinions or beliefs of any single people group. They are the beliefs that unite us in a common person and around a common purpose — namely,

Jesus Christ and his love for others, a love that transcends our own (at times) narrow, selfish concerns.

The "artistic" side of the equation will require you to navigate the many variables that must be tweaked and adjusted, depending on the specific individuals and people groups that make up your local body of believers. Like unique beans from around the world, people will come to your church from many different places and carry with them a variety of cultural experiences. All this should be taken into account before you simply turn up the heat and begin roasting! Indeed, the cultural dynamics of a multi-ethnic church are broad but subtle. Pastors and church planters must make it a priority to pursue cross-cultural competence if they hope to discover the nuances of each culture and their effect on the overall body of Christ. Ultimately, your effectiveness in ministering to a broad range of people within the church will hinge on your ability not only to understand but also to respect and rightly interpret for others various cultural perspectives related to Christ, the church, and the gospel.

TOGETHER WITH ALL THE SAINTS

As believers, we all recognize Jesus as our Lord and Savior, yet we often relate to him from the vantage point of our own particular background or heritage. Depending on our heart and our motives, this can be either a bad thing or a good thing. When our hearts are focused on loving God and people who are unlike ourselves — our diverse neighbors (Luke 10:25 – 37) — we are able to taste the hearty flavor of ethnic blends as God intends. Yes, when diverse people learn to walk, work, and worship God together in the local church, a better picture of Christ's love is visible to the world. It's precisely this kaleidoscope of love that Paul prays we would come to know through the church when he writes, "For this reason I kneel before the Father, from whom [every *patria* (people group)[1]] in heaven and on earth derives its name. . . . I pray that you, being rooted and established in love, may have power, *together with all the saints, to grasp how wide and long and high and deep is the love of Christ*, and to know this love that surpasses knowledge — that you may be filled to the measure of all the fullness of God" (Eph. 3:14 – 15, 17 – 19, emphasis mine).

Notice that Paul's prayer is for us to experience a power that is different from what is otherwise available when we gather together with believers who are most like us. It is a power that comes only when we are rooted and established in love "together with all the saints." In context, Paul is referencing the church at Ephesus, which was multi-ethnic. To reuse our coffee analogy, Paul is saying that God intends for us to know and enjoy the full flavor of ethnic blends and not merely to drink the same brand of coffee again and again!

CROSS-CULTURAL CHALLENGES

Of course, there are a variety of cross-cultural challenges that you'll need to overcome in order to create this fullness of flavor within your own local church. Even something as simple as preparing and producing a Sunday service at Mosaic requires us to consider issues of interpretation for first-generation Hispanic and Latino members of our church. We must create and project bilingual slides for Scripture reading and singing, print bulletins and handouts in both Spanish and English, and on many occasions have our worship leaders sing in Spanish. More than this, though, it requires us to spend our time and energy discipling individuals who have the heart and the capacity to reach beyond themselves for the sake of Christ. We need humble leaders who are willing to "do nothing from selfishness or empty conceit, but with humility of mind regard one another as more important than [themselves] ... [those who] do not merely look out for [their] own personal interests, but also for the interests of others" (Phil. 2:3 – 4 NASB) in order to build a healthy multi-ethnic church.

In some instances, cross-cultural sensitivities limit what we are able to do at Mosaic. For instance, in deference to those in recovery, we have chosen not to use real wine at our communion celebrations. And oil is now used instead of ash in our annual Ash Wednesday service, in deference to Hispanics and Latinos, to avoid any confusion as to the evangelical nature of our church. Through these adjustments and in other ways, we seek both to model and to cultivate a spirit of humility within the body. Likewise, local church pastors and planters pursuing the multi-ethnic vision must be willing to adapt their message and their forms for the sake of a diverse audience without compromising their core, theological convictions. Thankfully, Scripture provides both incentive and instruction to help us do this. Let's take a look at two familiar passages to see what they can teach us about overcoming cross-cultural obstacles in extending the love of God to others different from ourselves.

PAUL IN ATHENS (ACTS 17:16 – 34)

In this passage, Paul displays a high capacity for overcoming the obstacles of cross-cultural ministry. His speech, delivered in the midst of the Areopagus in Athens, is a classic example of an "incarnational" approach to ministry, that is, an approach that takes the gospel *through* a culture and not simply *to* a culture. How does Paul do it, and what can we learn from his methods?

In passing through the city, Paul observes that it is filled with idols (v. 16). However, rather than simply denouncing these false, culture-bound expressions of faith, Paul uses an inscription on an altar as a pivot point. According to verse 23, the inscription reads, "TO AN UNKNOWN GOD."

"What you worship in ignorance," he tells the diverse people of Athens — Jews, God-fearers, Epicurean and Stoic philosophers alike (vv. 17 – 18) — "[is] the God who made the world and all things in it … [the] Lord of heaven and earth, [who] does not dwell in temples made with hands; … [He] gives to *all people* life and breath … and He made from one man *every nation* of mankind…. [Therefore] God is now declaring to men that *all people everywhere* should repent" (vv. 23 – 30 NASB, emphasis mine).

I believe we can learn from the wisdom of Paul's approach here. Instead of condemning the things that divide us, the obvious differences we have, we must choose to focus on those points of connection that we share in common. And while Paul was attempting to relate to the nonbelieving citizens of Athens, this basic principle of cross-cultural communication can be applied to building a healthy multi-ethnic church.

At Mosaic, we begin with Christ, who is central to our common humanity and faith. It is his blood that has brought us near to one another and has broken down the dividing walls of hostility that so often and otherwise divide us. Yes, he is the one who calls us to be one "new man," a new household and dwelling in which God lives by his Spirit (Eph. 2:13 – 22). We also share a common point of connection with everyone attending our church in that we are all living in the United States, despite our differences. And while there is a long history of conflict between black and white Americans, the two groups share many common realities as citizens in this land. In a similar way, the deaf and blind among us represent two very unique cultures, regardless of the country they come from or the color of their skin.

Obviously, our ethnic, economic, and social distinctions are an ever-present reality and cannot be ignored as we seek to promote a spirit of inclusion within the body. Above all, we try to always remember that as believers, we have more in common with one another than we do with those outside the faith. As Christians, our unity in Christ is greater than the unity that comes from our ethnic or cultural heritage, greater even than the ties of blood that unite us with our earthly families (Mark 3:31 – 35). Indeed, we share "one body and one Spirit ... one hope when you were called — one Lord, one faith, one baptism, one God and Father of all, who is over all and through all and in all" (Eph. 4:4 – 6). Since we will share the same future together in eternity, why not start the party now?

Paul didn't just see the Athenians through the cultural lens of his Jewish heritage; he saw them for what they were: fellow human beings, a valued part of God's creation (Acts 17:26), groping for a God who was much closer than they realized. In leading a multi-ethnic church, you too must learn to interact with diverse others in a respectful, compassionate way. Sometimes they will come to you as sheep without a shepherd, lost and struggling to find God in desperation. At other times they will arrive with insight, experience, and gifts that will be an incredible blessing to you and the church. When God brings people from this second group to you, remember that your way is only *a* way and not *the* way to grow or develop the work. In humility, seek to learn from these gifted individuals and position them to become strong contributors in the development of your ministry.

Pursuit of cross-cultural competence should take into account economic realities as well. Recently I (Harry) have begun to pray regularly with a group of homeless men who gather daily in our church's parking lot. Steven Weathers, a campus/teaching pastor at Mosaic, has also joined me for this time. I have no doubt that some of these men are involved in some questionable activity. People come and go with "high" frequency throughout the day — if you catch my drift! The Little Rock police, who regularly patrol the area, scatter the group temporarily, but before long these men return to reclaim their same spot under the trees.

Like Paul among the Athenians, I began to wonder if the hand of Providence might be involved in all of this. There must be a reason why these men have chosen our parking lot in which to congregate, and I wondered if there might be some way in which I could reach them for Christ. So one day I just ventured into their midst and asked, "Hey, guys, can I pray with you?" Instead of being shocked or angry, they welcomed me to pray and have continued to invite me to join them. This has led to regular prayer meetings when Steven and I arrive for work each day. Some would call this an "organic church" or our efforts "missional." The men themselves call it "having church."

Most mornings Steven and I simply pray that the Lord would reveal himself; day after day we reiterate that there is nothing we can do to change their hearts. And so we call on the Holy Spirit to work within them. We ask God to show each man where he stands in relation to him. On some mornings we will even read a short Scripture verse and discuss it with them before we pray. Then they gather in a circle, remove their hats, and hold hands as we close the time together in prayer.

Some of the men have verbally expressed their faith in Christ, while others depart so quickly when we approach the group that it's obvious that they want nothing to do with us! But just as we've seen in Acts 17, when Paul preached to the Athenian philosophers, others continue to show interest in our message. In fact, several of these men have begun attending our worship services regularly and now have printed name tags awaiting them when they arrive, an indication of their membership at Mosaic if not yet in the kingdom of God.

PAUL TO THE CORINTHIANS

A second passage in which we find incentive and instruction for overcoming cross-cultural obstacles within the church is found in 1 Corinthians 9:19 – 23: "Though I am free and belong to no man, I make myself a slave to everyone, to win as many as possible. To the Jews I became like a Jew, to win the Jews. To those under the law I became like one under the law (though I myself am not under the law), so as to win those under the law. To those not having the law I became like one not having the law (though I am not free from God's law but am under Christ's law), so as to win those not having the law. To the weak I became weak, to win the weak. I have become all things to all men so that by all possible means I might save some. I do all this for the sake of the gospel, that I may share in its blessings."

The Incentive

What does Paul mean when he says he wants "to win as many as possible"? Does the "many" he's talking about refer to greater

CONNECTION AND COMMUNITY

Dana Baker, Director of Multicultural Ministries
Grace Chapel, Lexington, Massachusetts

I truly believe that what has happened at Grace Chapel is a work of God, a *kairos* moment where God, for his own sovereign purposes, has chosen us for this work—not because we have, as the apostle Paul says, anything with which to commend ourselves but simply because God has chosen us to be blessed in this way. And yet we have also needed to take intentional steps at key points to nurture what God is doing. As we transitioned from being an almost entirely monocultural church of people of western European descent, fifteen years ago, to a congregation now approaching 30 percent non-Anglo ethnicity, we have learned how important it is to listen to the voices of the people whom God has brought to our church and not, as leaders from the majority culture, try to figure it out for ourselves.

One of the most important steps we took was to design a focus-group study to which we invited fifty of our nonmajority culture leaders who reflected the breadth of diversity in our congregation—from all continents, 1.0s, 1.5s (arriving in the United States as children), 2.0s, multiple generations, and interracial couples. Out of that study arose some fundamental commitments that we follow to this day.

One of the most challenging of those has been the commitment to balance ethnic-specific ministry with integration into broader Grace Chapel ministries. For many people, transforming from attending a single-ethnic immigrant church to attending a multi-ethnic church can seem too wide a gap to cross. Sometimes the creation of single-ethnic fellowships will only perpetuate that gap within the confines of a church, because most activity continues to be centered on a specific cultural group. While separate-ethnic fellowships with ethnic-specific pastors are certainly appropriate for certain contexts, we have chosen a somewhat different path.

People at Grace Chapel are at very different stages in their cultural-identity development. While complete integration into the life of the church is our goal, we realize that for some, language can be a barrier to full participation. How does a person who speaks limited English, or even is merely perceived by either himself or those around him as having such a limitation, find a place of connection without being overwhelmed by all of the new cultural realities? While we are pursuing multiple avenues to help with the transition, like the recent introduction of language translation for our worship services, we have found our life communities (a variation upon a more traditional cell or small group model) to be one of the best solutions for achieving the balance we seek.

cont.

For those from 1.0 or 1.5 generations, studying the Word of God in their "heart" language is often of utmost importance. Being under constant pressure to think the right words, to risk not understanding what someone else is saying, or to not be understood oneself can be exhausting. Ethnic-specific life communities create safe places for study and connection. Yet with the support of that community, people can be encouraged toward greater involvement in other areas of ministry. Some may remain in these life communities for only a short while before moving into a multicultural life community near where they live. For others, this need for cultural connection may be ongoing.

Minority-culture ethnic leaders at Grace Chapel have sometimes made commitments to help those needing this kind of safe environment, even when they personally desired a more multicultural environment. But in making that commitment, they have often learned about their own potential for leadership in that same safe environment, so that when they do move out into the broader church community, they can do so with greater confidence and greater understanding of their own God-given potential.

numbers of people, or is Paul referring to the cross-cultural nature of the gospel and to his own desire to win many different, diverse people to Christ, to "save some" from every walk of life? I believe the context makes it clear that Paul is writing not only about winning more people to Christ but also about specifically winning more diverse people to Christ. To paraphrase 1 Corinthians 9:22 – 23, Paul is saying that he willingly extends and adapts himself to all people in order to "save some from as many people groups as I can beyond merely my own. Indeed, this is the power of the gospel: it breaks the dividing walls erected by human beings and sows peace among diverse people on earth as it is in heaven! Seeing diverse people come to know Christ through my efforts is a tremendous blessing" (see also Eph. 2:11 – 22).

It's unfortunate that these verses are often used to subtly promote the adoption of a mindset or methodology that encourages church planters to target a single people group. When we do this, we overlook the full context of the passage. It is true that Paul is declaring his passion to do whatever is necessary to reach many people with the gospel. Yet we must not forget that Paul wrote this passage to instruct believers in Corinth to be eager and willing to adapt themselves in order to extend the love of God, the gospel, to others no matter who they are or where they come from. In the broader context of the chapter, then, Paul is making a key point: he's not doing anything for himself or simply for the sake of his own ethnic group. He's not about material gain, earthly fame, or reward. Paul is serving Christ not only for the sake of those who are like him but also for the sake of those who are very different from him. Seeing diverse people come to the Lord by faith and, consequently, walking together as one in Christ and in his church is the blessing that Paul is excited to share with his readers (v. 23). The transferable truth is that we should have in us this same mindset as well.

The Instruction

This passage from 1 Corinthians also helps us at Mosaic to define three character traits that we look for in evaluating potential leaders.

1. You Must Surrender Your Rights (Preferences)

> Though I am free and belong to no man ...
> — *1 Corinthians 9:19*

When Paul says he is free in Christ, he is emphasizing that neither his worship nor his ministry are bound by the religious customs or cultural traditions of any single people group. Nor is he allowing some people to control him to the exclusion of others. Rather, he has freely surrendered his preferences for the sake of the gospel. Therefore Paul seeks first to understand diverse others and then to accommodate his ministry to meet their needs in order to win them to Christ.

From the beginning, this mindset has served to guide and govern decision making at Mosaic at all levels within the church. It's just who we are, part of our DNA. For in a multi-ethnic community, it is essential that we are willing to seek this common ground, laying aside our own preferences for the sake of the gospel.

2. You Must Extend Yourself to Others

To Those Most Like You

> To the Jews I became like a Jew, to win the Jews. To those
> under the law I became like one under the law (though I myself
> am not under the law), so as to win those under the law.
> — *1 Corinthians 9:20*

As we see in this verse and throughout Paul's ministry, he demonstrates a heart for his own people. He never shrinks away from the fact that he was born, and will always be, a Jew. Paul was fluent in the history, tradition, culture, customs, and mindset of his people, as well as the faith and practice of Jewish religion. In Philippians 3:5, he goes so far as to describe himself as a Hebrew of Hebrews!

Even so, God changed his heart, and he soon morphed from a proud, legalistic Pharisee into a humble, loving instrument of God. He began to look at his own people with great longing for them to come to know Christ — the true, long-awaited Messiah of biblical prophecy. In fact, Paul was so moved for his own people that he once wrote to the church in Rome, "I could wish that I myself were cursed and cut off from Christ for the sake of my brothers, those of my own race, the people of Israel" (Rom. 9:3 – 4).

Yes, Paul was so concerned for the salvation of his fellow Jews that he was willing to do anything to see them saved. His common practice, upon entering a city, was to go first to the Jews and into the synagogue with his message of Christ (Acts 14:1). As a missionary, he endured ridicule, beatings, threats, and suffering at the hands of the Jews, yet he still refused to stop speaking to them and reaching out to them with the gospel (as evidenced by his arrest in the temple in Acts 21:27 – 22:22). Nevertheless, he always made it a priority to minister first and foremost to his own people.

To be sure, there is nothing wrong with individuals who display a passion or concern to reach their own people with the gospel. Therefore, in spite of our desire to promote the multi-ethnic church, we must be sensitive toward and supportive of those with that passion and focus. We have no problem with Latinos wanting to worship in Spanish, conduct small groups in their own language, or ensure that the gospel is clearly presented to Spanish speakers. The problem arises when such passions direct the focus of the local church and minimize the vision of ethnic blends. In other words, targeting a particular group of people to the exclusion of others in a local church does harm to the overall body of Christ.

How else did Paul try to reach his own people? Among other things, he sought to remove barriers that kept them from experiencing the power of the gospel. In fact, Paul would willingly subject himself to the Jews' religious law and customs just to be heard (1 Cor. 10:27 – 33). Though he knew that such religious practices could not save people from sin, he adopted the practices to win Jews to Christ. By doing this, he was neither rejecting nor condemning his people. Instead he showed them respect and sought as many ways as possible to relate to them, short of committing sin, in order to influence their understanding of the truth about God, Christ, faith, and the church.

Obviously, there are many leaders and churches that do this quite well today. They effectively extend themselves to reach out to their own ethnic, economic, or social group for the sake of the gospel. When this is done successfully, large crowds of like-minded people are often won to Christ and gathered into churches. This is where we have seen the success of the homogeneous unit principle. But is this the fullness of God's vision for the local church? As we'll see, Paul intends for us to recognize that God's purposes go beyond reconciling individuals to Christ within our own people groups. To use his language, becoming a slave only to those of similar financial means is not what it means to become "a slave to *everyone*, to win *as many* as possible" (1 Cor. 9:19, emphasis mine). Becoming a slave to white-collar business professionals and highly educated people to reach them for Christ can be a good thing, but does it go far enough? The fact is, becoming a slave only to those who are most like you is only half the picture of God's vision for biblical community.

Without a doubt, serving a homogeneous congregation filled with people who are just like us has its challenges, but it is certainly much easier and more comfortable than ministering in a multi-ethnic environment. In spite of this, in this day, we are challenging pastors and church planters alike to embrace faith, courage, and sacrifice — as did the apostle Paul — and to lead local churches in the twenty-first century with a passion for all people that goes beyond what is popularly promoted or otherwise expected. Those who accept this challenge will see the supernatural power of God "do far more abundantly beyond all that we ask or think," so that the glory of God will be displayed "in the church and in Christ Jesus to all generations forever" (Eph. 3:20 – 21 NASB). Such leaders will prove to be like the men of Issachar (1 Chron. 12:32), understanding the times and paving the way for the local church to become more relevant and effective in the twenty-first century. So if you have not yet received an invitation, let me pause here to officially invite you: come and join us!

To Those Who Are Least Like You

> To those not having the law I became like one not having the law (though I am not free from God's law but am under Christ's law), so as to win those not having the law. To the weak I became weak, to win the weak. I have become *all things to all men* so that by all possible means I might save some.
>
> — *1 Corinthians 9:21 – 22 (emphasis mine)*

In these verses, Paul also reveals his heart for diverse others beyond the Jews, namely, the Gentiles. But in speaking of "the Gentiles" today, we practically forget that the term in Paul's time was recognizably multi-ethnic. In his day, it was a collective description for every other tribe, tongue, and people outside the nation of Israel. Jews speaking or writing of the Gentiles in the New Testament era would have been thinking of Romans or Greeks, of Samaritans and Ethiopians, Cypriotes, Cyrenians or Cretans, or even, more broadly, of Arabians, Africans, or Asians, such as surely occupied cities like Corinth, Ephesus, and Antioch. In fact, in New Testament times, Antioch was the third-largest city in the Roman Empire.

To get a feel for the relative size and diversity of Antioch, it might be helpful to contrast it with Houston, Texas, the third-largest city in the United States today. According to Mother Earth Travel, "The city's extreme industrial diversity has resulted in a cultural blend that is equally impressive. With over sixty primary languages spoken in the homes of Houston Independent School District families, Houston is one of the most ethnically diverse cities in the United States. It's been further estimated that an additional thirty languages are also spoken on a smaller scale. Residents typically have a broad knowledge of and respect for other world cultures and enjoy numerous cultural events every year.... Needless to say, ethnic diversity has also broadened the horizons in the restaurant world. The number of cultures and cuisines represented throughout Houston is both impressive and appreciated."[2]

From a surprisingly similar cross-cultural context, then, Paul challenges us in 1 Corinthians 9 to get beyond ourselves for the sake of others coming to know Christ. "Sure," he is saying, "I'm a Jew, but I'll walk with the Arabs to lead them to Christ; I'll work with the Africans until I find common ground through which to share the truth; I'll even worship with the Asians and show them the way." How might you apply Paul's words to your own context?

Those of us who are called to lead the church in the twenty-first century must be willing to do the same for the sake of Christ. As an Asian American at Mosaic, I must walk together as one in Christ with my African American brothers and sisters, pursuing relationships and cross-cultural competence to win more of them to Christ and, on a broader scale, to partner with them in meeting the unique needs that affect their personal and spiritual development as a people group. They, in turn, must be willing to work with Hispanics and Latinos at Mosaic to help impact that community as well. Likewise, our Hispanics and Latinos have been called to come alongside white Americans to create together an environment of inclusive worship where Christ can be found by those still in the demographic majority in the United States today.

So how can we become one with diverse others in the local church? It begins when we commit ourselves to the pursuit of cross-cultural competence, to taking the time to understand the cultural perspectives, history, and struggles of people groups outside our own. The goal of all this is not to get others to think, feel, or become like us, nor should we force the discussion. Rather, we must be patient in loving, serving, and giving ourselves to those who are different from us in order to establish relationships of transparency and trust. In time, God will bring to light more significant questions, needs, or hurts, and we can process these together. In the end, only God's Spirit can cleanse the mind, heal damaged emotions, and provide strength for the will to overcome the pain of negative past experiences rooted in racial or class prejudice. In addition, we must elevate diverse leaders who are able to model this same commitment to learning from others different from themselves. And organizationally, we must demonstrate inclusive thinking that strategically accounts for the needs and concerns of everyone involved, without showing favoritism for any one culture (James 2:1 – 9).

3. You Must Not Be Dogmatic

> I have become all things to all men so that by all possible means I might save some.
>
> — *1 Corinthians 9:22*

Finally, in this passage Paul shows us that he is ready to do whatever is necessary to win those who are different from him to

Christ and to his church. What does he mean, though, when he says that he will use all possible means to reach them?

From the context, and from an understanding of Paul's life and ministry, it's clear that he is saying he is willing to go anywhere, become like anyone, and do anything — short of committing sin — to reach diverse others with the message of Christ. To brew ethnic blends in our local churches, we must follow his example.

Embracing this attitude will be difficult for many of us because it leads to places of dependence and discomfort. It goes against everything we've been taught about leading from our strengths and minimizing conflicts.[3] Indeed, the gray areas of cross-cultural ministry can be confusing and complicated to navigate, especially for those who are prone to dogmatic thinking. Church leaders who are inflexible, or unwilling to think outside the box, will struggle with the frequent tension that is inevitable when leading a multi-ethnic church. Some may seek to spiritualize issues to mask their own insecurities or agenda, or they will want to narrowly define everything from the style of worship to the strategy for evangelism. More often than not, while these leaders are arguing for the "biblical" approach, their opinions will be rooted in their own personalities, past experiences, or cultural perspectives, to the exclusion of others who differ from them. Such people must not be allowed to control the direction of the whole.

I can tell you from our own experience at Mosaic that inflexible rigidity, in all its forms, is detrimental to the life and well-being of a healthy multi-ethnic church. Those who are unwilling to set aside their own preferences in deference to others will surely hinder the advance of the mission, as they will be unable to get beyond themselves for the sake of the whole. Often, you will recognize people with this mentality by their broad, generally negative references to diverse others. Rather than allowing people like these to determine your church's direction, look for leaders who are emotionally mature who will be able to navigate complex circumstances without compromising biblical truth.

FLEXIBILITY AND DISCERNMENT

Several years ago we allowed an avowed atheist to live in our facility. Dai Mitsutani was an international student from Japan who, prior to arriving in Little Rock, had never heard the name of Jesus.[4] Yet a few of our members at the time wanted to know why we would avail ourselves in such a way to a person who was not a believer. Initially they could see little value in his residency, and later they misinterpreted his reluctance to receive Christ as stubbornness or rebellion. Though allowing Dai to live in our facility reflected Mosaic's long-term strategy for representing Christ to the community in a

INCLUSIVE THINKING

Mont Mitchell, Senior Pastor
Westbrook Christian Church, Bolingbrook, Illinois

I've been at this a very long time, yet every day brings new challenges as we pursue the dream of being a multiethnic church. Often, for us, it's not so much the merging of cultures that is a challenge as it is the integration of those cultures and languages into the fabric of our community.

Even though we are committed to making our church as diverse as possible, we are often guilty of not being as thorough as we would like. I sometimes wish we could take a "pervasive-thinking pill" so that no matter what we are doing, designing, or planning, our thinking would automatically be about cultural and ethnic inclusiveness. We know this is how we should think—and often we do. But there are times when we slide back into our normal line of thinking, and we easily leave a culture out.

For example, since starting our Latino congregation, our teaching pastors have worked together on creating message series. We assess the spiritual needs of our body, seek the Lord's direction, and then craft our message series for the year. As we do, we regularly ask the following questions: How does this translate into the Latino context? How does this translate into Spanish from a language perspective? How might this series communicate truth to different ethnic cultures? We work hard at answering these questions, and we feel good about it. So we get an A for effort. But when it comes time to design the creative elements of the series for print, staging, and the like, we are sometimes guilty of erring on the side of the English language and Western thinking. We leave Spanish winsome way, they were uncomfortable with the situation for no other reason than that: it made *them* uncomfortable.

As a multi-ethnic church pastor and planter, you will face similar circumstances, requiring you to think creatively and exercise a flexible discernment without sacrificing your commitment to the Word of God. For instance, when you become aware that someone in your body is an undocumented immigrant, will you yet allow them to serve communion, lead worship, or teach a Bible study? On what grounds will you base your decision, one way or another?

In overcoming cross-cultural obstacles, then, the question becomes, How willing are you to put up with the issues, flaws,

off the graphics, or when we are designing the stage set, we forget to include elements of inclusiveness that might relate to people from other cultures our ministry touches. When we look at our efforts at inclusiveness based on this aspect, we have to give ourselves a C minus.

Or take, for example, when a new policy handbook or training manual is written. Do our people remember to be inclusive of all cultures? Not always. We won't be able to translate every piece of material into a hundred different languages, but we need to be proactive to do so for the ethnic groups we are reaching.

So here's the question: how do we think inclusively? We need a transformation of the mind. As Christ-followers, we want our minds to be transformed to the likeness of Christ. We also want our minds to be transformed to consistently think of ways to include the different ethnicities in our church.

In order to make sure that our minds are being transformed to think in an inclusive way, we often ask ourselves a series of questions: Why don't we always think about these things? Why does it have to be such hard work? Is the outcome worth all of the effort? Furthermore, does it really make a difference?

While there may be more questions than answers, we are committed to not only asking these questions but also trying to answer them. We most assuredly believe that it is worth the effort and sometimes the painful conversations, so we keep on keeping on!

and weaknesses of others seeking to walk, work, and worship God together as one with you? How willing are you to be honest about your own faults and failings? For in the end, the perfection of unity is found in overcoming such things so that, together with diverse others, we can be used of God in much greater ways than we might otherwise have been used on or with our own.

QUESTIONS FOR REFLECTION AND DISCUSSION

1. What cross-cultural challenges exist within your context of ministry? In what ways might your church be strengthened through greater diversity within your body? In what ways do the challenges within your context limit you from doing what you otherwise might wish to do or accomplish through your church in pursuit of ethnic blends? Pick one specific obstacle hindering your efforts and define one to three things you can do to overcome it.

2. How would you describe the general economic condition of your church? Are the majority of attenders impoverished, blue-collar, upwardly mobile middle-class, white-collar, or upper-class? Whatever the condition, how is your church extending the love of God to others outside this distinction? Consider James 2:1 – 4 and ask yourself this question: In all honesty, is my church preferential in its treatment of others based on economic class or social status? If you answered yes, how does this make you feel? What can or should you do about it?

3. Review and discuss the three character traits necessary for evaluating and choosing potential leaders that can be learned from Paul's instruction in 1 Corinthians 9:19 – 23 (pp. 157 – 63). When you consider the current leadership team serving your church, how do they measure up to these ideals? What about

you? As you look out on the landscape of your church's membership, are there potential leaders modeling these character traits who might be better positioned in the future to help your church pursue ethnic blends?

4. How flexible are you as a leader within your church when it comes to recognizing that your way is just *a* way and not necessarily *the* way to do things? How adept are you at navigating complex circumstances without compromising biblical truth? Where do you draw the line between conviction and compromise on one issue or another when others challenge you to see things in a different light? Is this a help or hindrance in relating to others cross-culturally?

5. What key thought, revelation, or insight will you take away from this chapter? What is God asking you to do in response?

Chapter 7

HUSKING THE OUTER SHELL

Overcoming the Relational Obstacles

How good and pleasant it is when brothers live together in unity!

— *Psalm 133:1*

A DAY IN THE LIFE

At a recent staff meeting, an initial discussion concerning a breakdown in communication escalated into a larger misunderstanding between Pastor Mark and Ronald Young, a key leader who was developing our enfolding process. Frustrations were aired on both sides of the swelling debate, and soon it was too late; words had been said, feelings had been hurt. Visibly shaken, Ronald abruptly left the meeting. I (Harry) followed him out to the parking lot, where I encouraged him to hang in there and work it out with Mark. Before he left, we prayed.

Following the meeting, Mark discussed the exchange with several of the other pastors on staff. What, he asked, could have been done differently, and how might we avoid such a situation in the future? It was a teachable moment for our team. We spoke to one another honestly, and all had something to learn from the discussion.

Later that afternoon, Mark called Ronald to apologize. For his part, Ronald graciously received the apology, expressed appreciation for the call, and asked Mark to meet with him on the following day. The two men met at a local Starbucks, where Ronald offered his own apology in person. What followed was a discussion — not an airing of offenses or grievances but a heart-to-heart conversation about life, ministry, and family. Indeed, they enjoyed the time together developing their relationship, growing closer, and getting to know each other better.

Several weeks later Mark and Ronald shared at a staff meeting how they had worked through the conflict and how their relationship had, in fact, been greatly strengthened because of each other's response. Following their encouraging words, we took some time to review conflict norms with our staff.[1]

Believe me, the resolution of this conflict was so encouraging to us all. For in some situations in the past when tensions have risen among leaders, differences of opinion have been taken personally. Sadly, several conflicts have ended with key leaders stepping down and leaving the church. This isn't the script we would have chosen to write for a ministry founded upon a vision to know God and make him known through the pursuit of unity!

Of course, relationships are important to the health and well-being of any church or leadership team. In a multi-ethnic church, however, relationships are critical to its success, given that so many of them must be developed with individuals of various cultures, adding a unique layer of complexity to the equation. Nevertheless, diverse relationships add a wonderful richness and depth to life and ministry. In this chapter, we'll consider some of the complexities of developing cross-cultural relationships and share with you some of the lessons learned from our experience. Let's begin with a definition of what we mean by "oneness," and consider four characteristics of relational unity.

ONENESS IS ...

1. *Oneness implies union.* Union: the act of forming one interdependent unit from two or more independent units, such as when a man and woman unite in marriage (Matt. 19:4 – 6; Eph. 5:25 – 33).

2. *Oneness implies identity.* Identity: when two or more independent units share a similar purpose or cause, identity is forged, such as in the case of an eye or a foot in supporting the human body (Rom. 12:4).

3. *Oneness implies harmony.* Harmony: the intentional focus of independent parts playing complementary roles, such as when two or more musical notes are played simultaneously to form a chord (Rom. 15:5).

4. *Oneness implies integrity.* Integrity: when a structure of one kind or another is sound and unimpaired, it is said to have integrity, such as in a set of support trusses under a bridge; integrity in a church allows the greater whole to carry the burdens or multiply the blessings of all those involved (1 Cor. 12:24 – 26).

Relational oneness, then, in an authentic multi-ethnic church will incorporate all of these elements. Yes, true unity will be more than just a slogan or mission statement; it will visibly reflect aspects of union, identity, harmony, and integrity.

LIVING WITH THE "MIS'S"

Make no mistake about it: in a multi-ethnic church, there is a 100 percent chance that at some point you *will* offend someone with a different ethnic or economic background — and you won't know how to resolve the tension. It's inevitable. In fact, every person on our staff has at one time or another said or done something that someone else has found offensive — and it has happened with uncommon regularity! In such moments, it can be very difficult not to take a comment or action personally. Indeed, the enemy seeks to exploit our every insecurity in order to create misunderstanding, destroy trust, and undermine the credibility of the gospel, and of the church, by causing division (Eph. 6:12).

Therefore, if you lead, or hope to lead, a multi-ethnic church, you (like Paul) must prepare to be misunderstood, misinterpreted, misrepresented, and misjudged as you relate cross-culturally with others. I call this "living with the mis's" — and it's no vacation! Here again, Acts 17 is instructive. As Paul shared the gospel with the people of Athens, notice that he too was:

1. Misjudged by some, who called him a "babbler" (Acts 17:18)
2. Misunderstood by some, who could not comprehend what he was saying (Acts 17:18)
3. Misinterpreted by some, who labeled the gospel of Christ "strange" (Acts 17:20)
4. Misrepresented by some, who sneered and mocked him (Acts 17:32)

In circumstances like these, our natural tendency is to grow hard-hearted toward those who push back at us. Or we go to the opposite extreme and become a people pleaser to avoid conflict and win approval. Neither extreme is appropriate or Christlike. We must learn to remain tenderhearted and gracious, even when sharing hard truths with others. Paul modeled this sort of persistence and patience as he ministered in Athens, looking for others who were hungry to learn and responsive to the message (Acts 17:34).

You must also be ready to extend grace and mercy to those who offend you. Remember that wounded people react in wounding ways. Many of them are driven by deep-seated insecurities, sensitivities, and loyalties of which they are largely unaware. Consequently, they live in a state of self-deception and in bondage to the hurts or regrets of their past. Mix in diverse social or cultural perspectives, and the resulting conflicts can get quite complicated. On the other hand, relationships that are committed to extending grace — when patiently nurtured — can be like mortar to the bricks, forming a sturdy foundation of trust and authenticity within a multi-ethnic church. A single act of forgiveness to someone of another culture who has offended you will manifest the power of Christ to break dividing walls before all who witness it, and establish a standard of humility within the church.

PROTECT THE PROCESS

I wish I could say that we've got all of this figured out by now. In truth, the current state of oneness in our church is often like the weather in central Arkansas — it can change in an instant, for better or for worse! Quite naturally, there are seasons in which everyone is on the same page, and times when they are not. As a leader of God's people, it is your responsibility to promote and protect a biblical process for conflict resolution that will help "keep the unity of the Spirit through the bond of peace" (Eph. 4:3). Don't give up when tempers flare and conflicts arise among diverse people within the church. Encourage those involved not to quit on one another. Again, your role is to ensure that unity is being rooted, established, and perfected among *all* the saints.

How can you do this? Begin by equipping your leadership in the art of conflict resolution as described in Matthew 18:15 – 17.[2] This is an all-important road map for resolving relational conflict and must be valued as a nonnegotiable first step. Some conflicts will get really messy and may even involve some of your top leaders. In times like these, you will need to stick to the process and resist the temptation to improvise. Encourage everyone involved to stay committed to the biblical course. Remind them of the things that unite them, and challenge the people who are directly involved in the conflict to try to work things out. Only when those directly involved cannot resolve a matter should you introduce a mediator. Though there is some risk in waiting, always encourage the offended person to go immediately to the offender when you first hear of someone raising a complaint against someone else.

In my opinion, pastors tend to get involved far too early in seeking to resolve relational conflicts within the church. To avoid this, take the time to encourage, train, and coach the more spiritually mature party in the dispute to offer forgiveness or receive it graciously for the sake of unity. Keep in mind that in many cases, those involved will not want you to know that a conflict even exists, so be careful with what you say and how you advise once you choose to get involved. Whenever a pastor in the church steps into a peacemaking role, the matter — no matter how insignificant — is instantly elevated in importance, because a third party is now engaged. Therefore do not rush to bring the matter to the attention of a governing board unless the conflict persists and begins to threaten the unity of individuals or of the church.

In addition to these suggestions, make sure you enlist and empower other gifted mediators within the body to play a significant role in Christ-centered conflict resolution. From the earliest days of Mosaic, we have relied on such individuals, who are trained and gifted in this way, and we have quickly turned some of the more delicate situations over to them. This allows those involved to resolve tensions within a more objective environment, where they don't have to worry about whether their pastor will take one side or the other.

To further promote a biblical process for conflict resolution, adopt conflict norms for your staff and at the highest levels of leadership within your church.[3] The norms should be written down and discussed with regularity until everyone is of one mind in the matter and agrees to live by them in seasons of relational uncertainty.

More often than not, we find that there is no one who is more right or wrong than another. Most conflicts are, rather, born out of inconsideration, misunderstanding, or insecurity. Often, everyone involved has something to apologize for, and mutual forgiveness is a common way of reaching reconciliation. Indeed, it's easy to love those who love you, but it's another thing altogether to love those who have hurt you! The width, length, height, and depth of the love of Christ that people are able to grasp and embrace is often directly related to the width, length, height, and depth of the hurt that they have been able to overcome through forgiveness, grace, and mercy. Even saints offend other saints, but where sin abounds, grace must abound all the more.

LOVE IS A VERB

As we've been saying, relational obstacles are an unavoidable reality in multi-ethnic ministry. Unity this side of heaven, therefore, is not found in the absence of conflicts but rather through a commitment of individuals to the Christlike resolution of conflicts. In the previous chapter, we asked, How willing are you to put up with the issues, flaws, and weaknesses of others? How you answer is critically important.

We've had to wash a lot of feet here at Mosaic — literally! In fact, Mark and I introduced foot washing as a practice in our congregation during our first Good Friday service in 2004. On that night, we decided to pick out two unsuspecting individuals from each of the small crowds rotating through various stations of the cross and wash their feet. By doing so, we were blessed to experience the power of this humble act, which breaks down our pride and brings blessing to those who are discouraged, weary, or in need of a tangible encounter with the presence of Christ. In subsequent years we have repeated the practice of foot washing in a variety of situations. In one instance, however, this simple, commemorative tradition became one of the most significant obstacles to relational unity I have ever encountered.

Amos Gray, a former youth pastor at Mosaic, and I come from two different worlds. Born and raised in Panke, Arkansas, Amos comes from an historic African American community — once on the outskirts of town — that is now surrounded by the white-flight suburbs of Little Rock. His ancestors can be traced to the days of slavery and include some of the first emancipated African Americans to ever settle in Arkansas as free men and women. "His people" have walked with God by faith in Christ for some seven generations!

I (Harry), on the other hand, trace my ancestry to rural, southern China in the 1850s. In fact, two of my great-great-grandfathers (maternal) were among the first Christian converts led to the Lord by Baptist missionaries. My relatives first arrived on

U.S. soil in 1896 and began crisscrossing the Pacific Ocean until my father, from Shanghai, and mother, from Guangzhou, met in Chattanooga, Tennessee, in the mid 1950s. As with Amos, faith in Christ runs deep in my family — six generations deep, since my own children have now come to know Christ.

Amos and I share a common faith and a common Lord. But in every other way we are just about as different as two men can be:

1. Amos was a collegiate-level athlete, but I was (and still am) a big techno-geek!
2. Amos likes hip-hop, while I like classical music. In fact, it took me several months to learn how to clap on the upbeat without looking like a discombobulated chicken!
3. Amos likes wings; I prefer egg rolls.

But I digress into stereotypes!

What began one day as an impromptu discussion I had with Amos about race relations soon turned passionate and personal. Amos spoke of his own frustrations in working at Mosaic and confessed that I had offended him in several ways: subtle looks and offhanded comments that had been perceived as condescending. In turn, I confessed my own perceptions of feeling wrongly judged by him and not feeling accepted as a brother in Christ. Unfortunately, that day our conversation was abruptly interrupted. We both walked away from the table with issues unsettled and feelings hurt.

The next day, as I read the powerful words of Christ in John 13, I came to the conclusion that I did not really know how to love Amos as Christ loved him (and as Christ loved me). The more I reflected on our heated discussion, the more I became convinced that Amos was, in all probability, just as perplexed as I was. So I called him on the phone and invited him to lunch, where I shared some of my thoughts from that morning. We both realized that if we could not figure out how to love each other in Christ, there was little hope that others at Mosaic would be able to do so. By the end of our time together, we were greatly encouraged by our discussion and felt that we had entered a new level in our relationship.

The following Sunday, since it was my turn to preach, I used the opportunity to share with the congregation all that I had been learning about Christ's new commandment (John 13:34). Despite my position as a pastor in a multi-ethnic church, I admitted that I really didn't understand how to love diverse others the way Christ had first loved me. I shared some of the details of my interaction with Amos earlier in the week and then asked Amos to come forward and share from his own perspective. Our message to the congregation was a visible witness of the new love we had discovered for one another as brothers in Christ.

But that was just the beginning. God had something else planned for our time that morning.

To be completely honest, I will admit that when I woke up that morning I had a strong sense that God was prompting me to do something to demonstrate my newfound love for Amos. In fact, I was pretty sure he wanted me to wash Amos's feet in front of the entire church at the conclusion of my sermon! I can assure you, I have never been more nervous before a worship service than I was that day. Leading up to the moment, I fought my pride with every ounce of strength I could muster; in the end, I had to will myself to do what God was asking of me. So after Amos finished his testimony, I asked him to remain with me on the platform and told him that Christ had, in fact, provided a tangible way of showing us how to love one another, "even as I have loved you."

Quite surprised, Amos resisted at first, seeing the stool, the pitcher, and the basin. But when Amos heard my voice starting to quiver and saw the tears flowing from my eyes, he knew that this was more than just a sermon illustration. As I washed his feet, Amos broke down, deeply moved within his heart. Soon the entire congregation was wailing. The Spirit of God moved in the hearts of people, and our morning service became a time of great healing for the church. Later we would learn that God used this single moment to propel other relationships within the church to an even deeper level of respect, admiration, and maturity.

Since that morning, I have washed the feet of many others at Mosaic too, both in good times and bad, sometimes in heartfelt humility and at other times when hurt feelings, raw emotions, and misunderstandings still lingered in the room. By way of practical advice, I can tell you that washing the feet of another in the midst of tension is not an easy thing to do. It is an act of submission and humility that reveals more of your own pride than you might otherwise imagine. Yet every single time that I have done so in the midst of conflict, it has defused anger and silenced the room. Every single time it has honored God.

Over the years, I've heard comments from others questioning whether the act of foot washing really translates to our own time and culture. Did Christ intend it to be just a metaphor, or was it something he desires us to practice as well? Rather than argue for one position or another, I will simply confess that I am compelled to wash the feet of others as a concrete illustration of Christ's love. Similar to communion and baptism, foot washing is an outward expression of an inner reality. We have found the practice to be useful in communicating the kind of attitude we want all members to display toward one another, especially in times of relational struggle. But it certainly is not the only way in which we can demonstrate love for others in a multi-ethnic church.

If you question the effectiveness of or the need for foot washing in your church today, I simply challenge you to try it. Be forewarned, however, that you will likely face a powerful internal struggle leading up to the moment, something you will need to overcome by God's grace if you want to truly experience such things with another individual as I've described. Embrace a spirit of humility, then, and don't worry about what other people may think—just do it!

AN OCEAN OF LOVE

During one fifteen-year period in my life, I was an avid guitar player. Once my three children were born, however, I found that

THE ELEPHANT IN THE ROOM

Efrem Smith, Senior Pastor
Sanctuary Covenant Church, Minneapolis, Minnesota

Seven years ago our church formed with a desire to be intentionally evangelical, multicultural, and urban. Even today our vision is to ignite a reconciling movement, and our purpose is to change the face of the local church by reconciling people of the city to God and one another. With this in mind, we have also worked intentionally to be a reconciling community that works to dismantle the walls of race and class that so often divide. To accomplish this, we knew that we would need to do more than just gather together on Sunday mornings. And though a Sunday morning, multicultural experience in worship is still somewhat of a rarity and so powerful in and of itself, achieving reconciliation takes other types of personal engagement.

After conversations and prayer over potential ministry models, we landed on community groups as a major strategy for developing reconciling relationships within our church. Our first step, then, was to train community group leaders. Yet in studying various small group ministries in the past, it seemed that many models were built on connecting with others of similar ethnicity, economic status, or educational background—especially when they were based in homogeneous congregations. So to overcome this challenge, we began training leaders through a Leaders' Orientation Initiative (LOI) that included a Bible study on race and reconciliation. Our goal through the initiative was to equip potential leaders to develop and lead community groups that would be multi-ethnic.

Teaching from the second chapter of the book of Acts, I instructed the diverse men and women attending the LOI about the Christ-centered community that learned together, shared meals together, and met in homes together. I also talked with them about the obstacles that might keep us from developing multi-ethnic community groups. And in that moment I began to talk about racism. As soon as I brought it up, many of the African Americans began to speak with passion. Some told stories of growing up in the Deep South, others of being followed around the mall by security officers or in stores by employees when they had merely come in, like everyone else, to shop. The interesting thing is that while the African Americans were sharing such things, most of the white people in the room remained silent. Finally a white woman spoke up and said, "I thought racism was over." Awkward silence followed; you could feel the tension in the room.

I then shared a similar story from my own experience. Once I was on a flight and was the only African American that day who was seated in first class. Twice the flight atten-

cont.

dant (a white woman) came by to ask if I was sure I was sitting in the right seat. She didn't bother to ask any of the other people sitting around me a similar question (because they were all white). When I finished telling the story, another white woman at the LOI tried to downplay the incident by wondering aloud if this was really racism. Needless to say, the night ended with some unspoken tension between some of the people in our church, causing me to wonder if multi-ethnic small groups could ever be a reality for us!

Later I brought this issue to our elder board, seeking some input. One of the solutions we came up with was to sponsor a one-day forum on authentic dialogue. We brought in a group of facilitators who helped us work through ways to have healthy and authentic dialogue about issues of race. We talked and later prayed for the ability to listen to one another and to really digest one another's stories. We didn't solve all of our issues that day, but the forum did begin to move us in the right direction. Another initiative that has helped us relationally is called the Invitation to Racial Righteousness, a day-and-a-half experience facilitated by the Department of Compassion, Mercy, and Justice of the Evangelical Covenant Church (www. covchurch.org). We have found that bringing a third party in to facilitate healthy discussion can help a multi-ethnic church grow as a reconciling community.

there simply was not enough time to pursue music as I did before. For years my Ovation guitar sat idle in the back of my closet. Then, several years ago, my two oldest daughters began to show an interest in playing. Soon my wife, Melanie, had conspired with a member of our church, Jason Truby, and together they convinced me to pick up the guitar again and take some lessons! Now, Jason not only is a fantastic guitar teacher but also a world-class guitar player and platinum-selling recording artist, the former lead guitar player for the Grammy Award – winning band P.O.D. In just one lesson, then, I learned how little I actually knew about playing the guitar!

At the time, Jason explained to me that the guitar is like an ocean. Most guitar players, he said, never wade in more than ankle deep. Over the next several months, then, he taught me styles, scales, techniques, and chords that I had never known before. And

I soon realized that in my previous fifteen years of playing, I too had only dipped my toe in the water.

Jason's metaphor of the ocean is helpful when I think about the work God has done at Mosaic. During the first few years of our church, we spent a lot of our energy casting vision and inviting anyone who was willing to go swimming with us in the multiethnic ocean. Thankfully, some jumped into the uncharted waters headfirst and still love swimming with us to this day. Some others only dipped their toes in the water before running back to the beach. Still others today stand on the shore and watch, wondering if (and in some cases, even hoping that) Mosaic will fail.

Looking back, I know that those of us in the water at the time thought we were swimming deep. Soon we realized, however, that we were still in the shallows and that there was an entire ocean of love yet to be explored!

I believe that as Paul thought about the multi-ethnic church in Ephesus and prayed for it, he had a similar picture in his mind — a realization that the love of God which the church was experiencing was just a small part of what was out there, farther out to sea. Paul writes, "I pray that you, being rooted and established in love, may have power, together with all the saints, to grasp how wide and long and high and deep is the love of Christ, and to know this love that surpasses knowledge — that you may be filled to the measure of all the fullness of God. Now to him who is able to do immeasurably more than all we ask or imagine, according to his power that is at work within us, to him be glory in the church and in Christ Jesus throughout all generations, for ever and ever! Amen" (Eph. 3:17 – 21).

In this passage, Paul describes for us a love so vast that it would take many lifetimes to explore! This is the kind of love that can be found and experienced in a multi-ethnic church, a love that flows from an experiential understanding of the love of Christ and surpasses human comprehension or expectation (Eph. 3:20). Note that as he prays, Paul challenges the Ephesians to explore this ocean of love and together *with all the saints* discover its treasures. It is a challenge he extends to us today as well.

COMMANDED TO LOVE

Christ commands and expects that we extend love in four directions:

1. Love God (Matt. 22:37; Mark 12:30; Luke 10:27)
2. Love your neighbors (Matt. 5:43; 19:19; Mark 12:31)
3. Love your enemies (Matt. 5:44; Luke 6:27 – 35)
4. Love one another (John 13:34 – 35)

It is interesting to note that the first three of these commands, rooted in Old Testament law, are given new clarity through Christ's life and teaching. In fact, Christ fulfilled both the spirit and the letter of the law in each case and provided a powerful example for us to follow. However, Jesus describes the fourth of these commands as a completely new commandment, and it was one that he had not, in fact, delivered to his disciples until the night before he died. Practically speaking, I believe it's this new commandment that holds the key to forging cross-cultural relationships of transparency and trust between believers of various ethnic or economic backgrounds within the church. To get a better handle on this, let's briefly consider the four intended recipients of love.

Who Is God?

Among the more creative ideas introduced in the bestselling fictional book *The Shack* are the representations of God the Father as an African American female, of Jesus Christ as a Middle Easterner, and of the Holy Spirit as an Asian woman. Certainly, the book is a work of fiction and was not intended to be a theological treatise. Still, there is a theological error in the book that happens to highlight an essential truth about the way we come to know God through Jesus Christ.

The Bible is clear in teaching us that God is most accurately represented in human form only by one person, Jesus Christ. According to Hebrews 1:3, Jesus Christ is the exact representation of God's being. It's only as we seek to understand and know

Christ that we are able to find answers to the deeper questions about God, such as, Who is God? What is he like? How does he relate to me? Jesus Christ is the answer to these questions! He both clarifies and models who God is and what it means to love him with all our heart, soul, mind, and strength — the first and foremost command, according to Matthew 22:36 – 38. Indeed, our understanding of God is both limited and informed by our understanding of Christ. It is only by following Christ's example, giving the Father full control of our lives, and dying to ourselves, that we can fulfill this command.

Who Are My Neighbors?

In Christ we also discover who our neighbors are and what it means to love them. In most cases, we find it easy to pursue peace and practice love with those closest to us: our family and friends and those with whom we have things in common (race, class, or education). That's one reason why the homogeneous unit principle is so effective in growing churches quickly. But Christ expects more of us than simply loving those who are like us! We have been commanded not only to love our own but also to love our neighbors as ourselves — as we would our own family. For as Jesus said, " 'Love the Lord your God with all your heart and with all your soul and with all your strength and with all your mind'; and, 'Love your neighbor as yourself' " (Luke 10:27).

Immediately following his words in this passage, Jesus is asked, by a man seeking to justify himself, "Who is my neighbor?" (Luke 10:29). It is to this question, that Jesus responds by telling the parable of the good Samaritan.

To understand the full context and meaning of the parable, it is important to recall that Samaritans were the descendents of the Northern Kingdom of Jews conquered by the Assyrians in 722 BC. Their once-pure Jewish bloodline had been corrupted through intermarriage with the Assyrians, and their worship of Yahweh corrupted through the assimilation of pagan beliefs and ritual. Consequently, the Jews living in Judea at the time of Christ, the very audience to whom Jesus was speaking, hated the Samaritans.

The primary purpose of the parable, then, is to clarify just whom Christ has in mind in speaking of a neighbor. And as we study the parable closely, we learn that "my neighbor," according to Christ, is not only someone in need but also someone *who is not like me*. More specifically, he teaches that a neighbor is someone we might naturally avoid, disregard, or even despise based on ethnic origin. For the neighbor in the parable was a Jew, and the one who loved him as himself, like one of his own, was an otherwise despised yet good Samaritan. This is not by coincidence. The practical implication for the Jews listening to Jesus was that they would have to learn to love not only one another but also those outside their own culture, with genuine, sacrificial love apart from distinctions. Indeed, if a Jew wanted to fulfill the command to love his neighbor as himself — the second-greatest command, according to Matthew 22:36 – 39 — he would have to learn to love like the Samaritan in the parable and, more than that, to love Samaritans in obedience to Christ.

Who Are My Enemies?

Nowhere in the Old Testament are we commanded to hate our enemies. Yet in the Sermon on the Mount, Christ must clarify a hypocritical misinterpretation of the religious leaders in his day (Matt. 5:43 – 44). Jewish leaders were teaching that as long as the people loved their neighbors (essentially, each other), they were free to hate those who treated them badly (their enemies). In Jerusalem at the time of Jesus, this meant the Romans and, more broadly, the Gentiles. Surprisingly, Jesus taught his fellow Jews that they should love their enemies, regardless of how they were treated in return.

We all know that it is fairly easy to love those who love us in return. There is nothing unnatural or remarkable about this type of love. Jesus mentions in Matthew 5:46 – 47 that even nonbelievers do this! Yet what will separate his followers from the rest of the world is their desire and God-given ability in Christ to love those who are different, who oppose them and hate them, even their enemies. Yes, Christ commands us to love others — regardless of personal preference. Toward those who persecute us, take advantage of us, or otherwise treat us badly, our response should always be the same: we are to love them as Jesus does. Not only are we to love our enemies, but we are to pray for them as well (Matt. 5:44).

Through our prayers and actions, we are called to love all people with the love of Christ. By this uncommon, unnatural love, the world will witness the power of God and give glory to him.

Who Are My Fellow Disciples?

On the night before he died, Jesus spoke to his disciples, saying, "A new commandment I give to you, that you love one another, even as I have loved you, that you also love one another. By this all men will know that you are My disciples, if you have love for one another" (John 13:34 – 35 NASB).

At first glance, you might wonder, "This can't be a new command. Certainly Christ had instructed his disciples to love one another before that fateful night?" But, surprisingly, this *was* a new command for them. For until that moment, Christ had not once (according to the biblical record) spoken directly to his disciples about the type of love they were to have for one another, their fellow disciples. So when Jesus delivered this *new* commandment, he was not merely suggesting a great idea. He meant for them to receive it as an addition, of equal importance, to the Ten Commandments given to Moses. It was also intended to serve as a promise of the empowerment that would come from the Holy Spirit, who would enable them to live out this command in their life and witness. Through Christ, then, we see another dimension of love: the ability to love fellow believers in an entirely new and different way. When we love one another as Christ loved us, we are told, the world will be attracted to him and to his church. Yes, the world will come to know him as we do.

EMOTIONAL HEALTH

Peter Scazzero, Senior/Lead Pastor
New Life Fellowship Church, Queens, New York City

Twenty-three years ago, when my wife and I planted New Life Fellowship, we chose Elmhurst/Corona, Queens, as a strategic location for the church due to the fact that individuals from more than 120 nations live in the area. In addition, the neighborhood consisted then, as it does now, of poor, working, and middle-class New Yorkers. So while we recognized the benefits of such a location and desired to bridge the racial, cultural, and economic barriers for the sake of Christ, we underestimated the suffering this commitment would require of all of us in leadership.

For instance, I soon realized that our evangelical discipleship/spiritual-formation model was too superficial to bring about the kind of in-depth transformation we would need to live in authentic community. There were tensions between Asians and African Americans, Columbians and Puerto Ricans, Arabs and Jews, Filipinos and Chinese, as well as Haitians and Dominicans, just to name a few. In fact, I remember one young Chinese American woman who left our church after being hurt and overwhelmed by conflicts and the direct approach of people from other cultures interacting in her small group.

Barriers of economic class and educational status also loomed large in our midst. For instance, educated African Americans struggled with other African Americans who embraced a "hood" mentality, and Asians, with their rich legacy of love for education, had great difficulty in embracing the large number of high school dropouts who now attended our youth group. In addition, middle-class Latinos struggled to empathize with Latinos who remained stuck in a cycle of poverty and dependence. Whites also struggled to embrace being minorities, many of them experiencing this for the first time.

We also underestimated the worldwide scope of racism based solely on the color of skin. For example, I learned that the darker one's skin in Latin America, the generally lower he or she remained in social standing. In fact, part of the reason why our Spanish congregation split in the early years was due to tensions between lighter-skinned and darker-skinned Latinos. We also had to consistently remind immigrants that they were now part of the American church. Biblically, they could not ignore the history of slavery and racism. We challenged them to participate in reconciliation efforts. Most preferred, at least initially, to ignore this call and move up the ladder of the American dream.

Key early decisions, then, enabled our church to grow into a congregation where individuals from more than sixty-five nations are involved today. We mentored peoples from a variety of cultures, focused on our common mission, and remained committed to the passionate worship of Jesus. And over time we slowly built an elder board, pastoral staff, and worship team that reflected our diversity.

Yet in our case, significant breakthrough came only when we began integrating emotional health and contemplative spirituality into our discipleship model fourteen years ago.

A spiritual formation paradigm that included emotional health began, for us, with a commitment to break the power of our past. Like Abraham, we responded to the invitation to leave our families, cultures, races, and countries behind to become part of the new family of Jesus (Mark 3:31–35). We also learned to lament our losses—like David, Job, and Jeremiah. We realized that whites, for example, needed to grieve their own losses if they were going to empathize with the losses of immigrants and minorities. And we began to value the characteristics of loving well and brokenness as true measures of maturity, instead of knowledge, gifts, or anointing.

We then called our people to leave the contemporary, consumer church model so prevalent in the West for a more radical spirituality modeled after the Desert Fathers from North Africa. We moved our membership to a "Rule of Life," invited people to contemplative practices such as Daily Offices and Sabbath keeping, and began a strong emphasis on silence and solitude. In so doing, we intentionally left what I typically call "American Christianity" for a radical pursuit of the person of Jesus. In other words, we united around a passion for him.

Our culture and city continue to change, and we at New Life continue to learn. But God has opened up a unique door through the building up of multi-ethnic churches to demonstrate the power of the gospel in the twenty-first century. And I, for one, could not imagine doing anything else!

To show his disciples the type of love he was talking about, Jesus knelt to wash their feet, reinterpreted the Passover meal so that it might continually remind them of his sacrificial love, and prayed that they would be one. These are just a few of the ways in which he demonstrated the kind of love he wanted his followers to show one another. On the night before he died, he even washed the feet of the one who would betray him! Imagine the impact such an act would have on these men for years to come, whenever they would think about the events of that evening and those events that soon followed.

To be clear, there is no biblical license that allows us to limit our love based on who a person is, what they look like, the color of their skin, how they act, where they were raised, the amount of money they make or contribute, whether they can speak English, whether they have an accent, their educational experience, their familial pedigree, their life experience, their political views, the square footage of their home, the neighborhood in which they live, the tree under which they sleep, or the kind of car they drive. Obviously, I could go on. The point is that those who have received the gift of God's Spirit are not only enabled to love diverse others but also commanded to love them in obedience to Christ. Therefore, we can and should extend love to all people through relationships in the church because the hearts of all those *in Christ* are now filled with the same unlimited, sacrificial, and unconditional love that first was given to us. And Jesus expects us to extend this love to one another for the sake of the gospel, beyond the distinctions of this world that for too long have kept the local church divided and segregated along ethnic and economic lines.

While there is no way we could ever master all that Jesus has shown us concerning love, we can and should die (to ourselves) trying. After all, on the night before he was crucified, Jesus prayed not that we would be perfect but that we would be "perfected in unity" through our love for one another (John 17:23 NASB).

Loving those who do not reciprocate your love is just about the hardest thing you will ever be called upon to do. I sometimes wonder, "How can our people live out the principles I have only just begun to discover?" The truth is that we cannot expect others to give to one another what we as leaders do not embrace or possess ourselves.

TRANSCENDENT LOVE

I've had many mentors throughout my life, but one of my favorites is fellow Mosaic Otto Helweg. Otto was a retired engineering professor with a seminary degree. We would start our weekly time together with a short tutorial in New Testament Greek and would progress into a deep theological or culturally relevant discussion. Sadly, Otto passed away suddenly in the fall of 2008. He was a gift to me and the body of Mosaic.

Another favorite mentor of mine at Mosaic is Ronald Young. Now, Ronald is very detail-oriented and able to see the church systemically. A former pastor himself, Ronald evaluates my latest sermon, asks about my family, and probes to find out where I am with God. His experience and godly wisdom always leave me encouraged and feeling unconditionally loved.

Now, Ronald is an African American, Otto was of German descent, and as you know, I am an Asian American: 100 percent Chinese. But the amazing thing is that it really doesn't matter one bit. Ronald, Otto, and I — we are family in Christ!

There is no substitute for healthy relationships that transcend race and class within the local church. In the twenty-first century, such relationships, and the churches in which they are forged, will likely provide the most credible witness of the love of God to people living in an increasingly diverse and cynical society. But there remains a very real threat to unity — a threat that perhaps, more than any other, is the single greatest challenge you will face in pursuit of ethnic blends. As you'll see in the next chapter, it is spiritual in nature, and it is the final, most potentially destructive obstacle you'll need to overcome to successfully grow and lead a healthy multi-ethnic church.

QUESTIONS FOR REFLECTION AND DISCUSSION

1. Review and discuss the definition of oneness as provided in this chapter. In what other ways might you define or describe oneness to someone else? Provide examples to illustrate your points. How can such understanding be used to build a healthy multi-ethnic church?

2. When was the last time you were misjudged, misunderstood, misinterpreted, or misrepresented by another person? How did it make you feel? How did you handle it? What did you learn from the experience? In what ways have you been shaped by it?

3. How defined or developed is a biblical process for personal reconciliation after conflict in your church? In what ways do you hold others accountable or have you personally modeled leadership in this regard? Have you ever washed the feet of someone else who has hurt or offended you in some way, whether privately in front of a few or more publicly before the church? What did you experience in doing so? In what other ways might you set an example for others?

4. Review and discuss Christ's teaching, his commands, on the subject of love as outlined in this chapter. Which one of these commands is the easiest for you to obey? Which one is the hardest? Why do you think this is so?

5. What key thought, revelation, or insight will you take away from this chapter? What is God asking you to do in response?

Chapter 8

STRANGE BREWS

Overcoming the Spiritual Obstacles

Destructive forces are at work in the city; threats and lies
never leave its streets.

— Psalm 55:11

A FRONTAL ASSAULT

Soon after the public birth of Mosaic in March of 2002, we were
feeling rather good about where things stood. We had landed a
permanent location for Sunday worship, an increased number
of people were attending from week to week, and Harry Li had
just joined our staff. Laypeople too were getting involved as ser-
vant leaders, including one relatively young woman who was the
mother of two small children. In fact, Shelly (not her real name)
had stepped up to lead our fledgling women's ministry with an
enthusiasm and competence that bode well for its future development. By that fall, some fifty women were already signed up for
small group involvement and Bible study. Shelly had even created
an individualized packet of Scripture verses for these women to
memorize, and they were doing so with a passion.

One day Shelly provided me (Mark) with a list of small group
leaders and members for my review, just prior to announcing them
to the ladies. Everything seemed in order, except for the placement of one woman whom I knew to be working through issues
of addiction. Since she was slightly on the fringe, I knew that she

was one who could go either way in terms of commitment. Consequently, I felt that she would be better placed in a group led by my wife, Linda, with whom she had already developed a strong friendship and was meeting on a weekly basis.

Calling Shelly, I recommended the change while providing a small measure of explanation without violating confidentiality. It was a simple change, the kind of thing I have recommended to staff on many occasions throughout the years and in a variety of situations, without incident. This time, however, I could tell that Shelly did not take the suggestion very well. In fact, I sensed a very strange and sudden change in her demeanor, even over the phone. During our conversation, she seemed to morph into someone I did not recognize; she was no longer the supportive person I had come to know and appreciate.

To be clear, it wasn't that she was confused by my request or somehow needed further explanation and affirmation. No, this was something altogether different, and I was at a loss to understand what was happening as Shelly began to speak to me in a judgmental and condescending tone. She said that she had spiritual authority in the matter, having "prayed day and night over the placement of each woman," and added, "I am confident that God has confirmed my decisions." She went on to accuse Linda too of trying to undermine her leadership in the matter. Beyond this, she began to speak to others in the church about the situation, making false accusations about my intentions, spreading misinformation about my wife, and ultimately painting herself as a victim of heavy-handed pastoral control.

Needless to say, this was quite an ordeal for a small, young congregation, and eventually we had to bring the matter before the only other elder in the church at that time beside myself. At that meeting, Linda and I made sincere apologies for any misunderstanding or confusion my initial input may have caused. On the other hand, Shelly saw no need to apologize, refusing to recognize that her response was in any way inappropriate or to take responsibility for misleading others in the church. Rather, she continued to insist that the Holy Spirit was standing with her in the matter, and she insinuated that I was leading the church according to my own agenda in opposition to the will of God. In short, she tried to turn others against me and Linda to undermine trust within the body. Thankfully, she did not fully succeed.

Following the meeting, Shelly and her family abruptly left the church. But the damage had been done. Through her lies and rumors, she had sown a measure of doubt and distrust that would soon lead to several other families leaving. Sadly, this incident would not be the last time we felt the onslaught of "spiritual forces of wickedness in the heavenly places" (Eph. 6:12 NASB) attacking us personally, or the church corporately, through individuals we had come to know and love.

I realize that such things occur in every church and ministry. Unfortunately, my story is not unique or uncommon. I simply mention it here because I later learned some additional details about Shelly from a very informed, confidential, and respectable source who also attended Mosaic in those days. This man informed me that Shelly had "been sent" specifically to the church for just such a time and purpose, to create distraction, to destabilize the fledgling work. The conversation was like something out of a Frank Peretti novel.[1] He told me that he spoke from firsthand knowledge, and he clearly implied that Shelly was not the only one who had come into the church for such a purpose. In fact, he led me to believe there might still be some attending! Given this man's character and vocation, he was someone I had no reason to doubt.

Now, I'm not the kind of person who looks for demons behind every rock. But there was no doubt in my mind that day, as I spoke to this friend, that there was something about our experience with Shelly that was truly demonic. As I mentioned, it was some of the earliest evidence that Linda and I were now engaged in a spiritual war.

Overcoming the spiritual challenges and inevitable attacks that come with the territory of multi-ethnic church leadership requires that you stay intimate with Christ, focused on your mission, and personally alert, conscious of the fact that Satan's desire is to destroy you and your family through persecution, false accusation, temptation, and discouragement. Indeed, his forces will seek to destroy a multi-ethnic church before it ever takes root, by destroying its leaders, discouraging its people, and dimming their vision. Ultimately, the goal of our spiritual enemy is to thwart the evangelistic power of unity so wonderfully manifest when diverse people walk, work, and worship God together as one in Christ.

Since the incident with Shelly, I have come to realize that pursuit of the multi-ethnic church represents a very bold and frontal attack on Satan and his kingdom. More specifically, it represents a direct threat to the strongholds of racism and human hatred long taken for granted by rulers and authorities, the powers of this dark world and spiritual forces of evil in the heavenly realms (see Eph. 6:12) who have used such weapons to divide and conquer humanity in unholy rebellion against God through the centuries. If we stop and think about it, and accept what the Scriptures teach, this should come as no surprise to us. In fact, there are at least two specific passages that serve to forewarn multi-ethnic church pastors and planters of spiritual battles ahead. Let's take a moment to look at them now.

PEACEMAKING AND PERSECUTION

In Matthew 5:1 – 12 (a passage commonly referred to as the Beatitudes), Jesus promises *something* for all of those he describes as "blessed." For the poor in spirit, theirs is the kingdom of heaven (v. 3); those who mourn will be comforted (v. 4); those who are meek will inherit the earth (v. 5); those in pursuit of righteousness will be satisfied (v. 6); those who are merciful will receive mercy (v. 7); and those who are pure in heart will see God (v. 8). Notice in the next verse, however, that Jesus promises *someone* to those who, like him, pursue peace among people: "Blessed are the peacemakers, for they shall be called sons of God" (v. 9 NASB). In other words, the reward of a peacemaker is not something but someone, namely a personal identification with the very heart and mission of God's Son, Jesus.

Have you ever wondered why Jesus promises someone (himself), and not something, to the peacemakers?

Like the Prince of Peace, peacemakers are those who will themselves to live out the implications of relational harmony that accompany the message of the gospel. Peacemakers intentionally pursue unity for the sake of the gospel as they seek to walk "worthy of the calling" they have received (Eph. 4:1 – 3; see also John 17:20 – 23). And since they, like Christ, proclaim a message of reconciliation — first between God and man, and second between man and man — they are rightly called sons of God.[2]

But peacemaking is never easy. In fact, have you ever noticed that the next three verses speak of persecution? Jesus goes on to say, "Blessed are those who are persecuted because of righteousness, for theirs is the kingdom of heaven. Blessed are you when people insult you, persecute you and falsely say all kinds of evil against you because of me. Rejoice and be glad, because great is your reward in heaven, for in the same way they persecuted the prophets who were before you" (Matt. 5:10 – 12).

So, immediately following his blessing of peacemakers, Jesus speaks of the certainty of persecution, insults, and false accusations. As a peacemaker, Jesus was surely thinking of his own life and ministry, anticipating the conflicts and persecutions he would soon encounter. Yes, peacemaking is hazardous work and the path of a peacemaker is mined with earthly hardship.

With this in mind, multi-ethnic church pastors and planters who expect a blessed reward in identifying with the life and work of Christ should be prepared for a measure of spiritual and earthly persecution as well.

A COLLECTIVE STRUGGLE

A second passage of Scripture that also warns multi-ethnic church pastors and planters of spiritual battles ahead can be found in chapter 6 of Paul's letter to the Ephesians. Before turning there, however, let's briefly consider the theme and context of the entire letter.

Simply put, this letter is written to explain and promote the unity of the local church for the sake of the gospel. As we consider the general outline of the book, keep in mind that the church at Ephesus was multi-ethnic, consisting of both Jewish and Gentile believers (Acts 19:17; 20:21). Understanding the multi-ethnic nature of the church at Ephesus is essential to grasping Paul's theme and understanding his instruction.[3]

Paul first *describes* the reality of an individual believer's unity with God the Father, made possible through his prior choice of us and our faith in him (Eph. 1:4–5, 11, 13). In chapter 2, Paul next describes the sufficiency of the finished work of Christ, "who has made the two [groups, namely Jews and Gentiles] one and has destroyed the barrier, the dividing wall of hostility [that has historically existed between them].... His purpose was to create in himself one new man out of the two [groups], thus making peace, and in this one body to reconcile both of them [Jews and Gentiles] to God through the cross, by which he put to death their [historic] hostility" (Eph. 2:14–16). Notice that Paul uses a variety of metaphors to define the newfound oneness of both Jew and Gentile in Christ and in the church (contextually, the local church at Ephesus). The two groups are now described as "one new man" (v. 15), "one body" (v. 16), "God's household" (v. 19), a "whole building" and one "holy temple" (v. 21).

In chapter 3, then, Paul *declares* that this oneness of believing Jews and Gentiles in the local church is "the mystery made known to me by revelation ... the mystery of Christ, which was not made known to men in other generations as it has now been revealed by the Spirit to God's holy apostles and prophets ... that through the gospel the Gentiles are heirs together with Israel, members together of one body, and sharers together in the promise in Christ Jesus" (Eph. 3:3–6). They are called to be one in Christ and in his church so that the manifold wisdom of God will "be made known to the rulers and authorities in the heavenly realms" (v. 10). They are called to be one in order that they, "being rooted and established in love, may have power, together with all the saints, to grasp how wide and long and high and deep is the love of Christ, and to know this love that surpasses knowledge — that you may be filled to the measure of all the fullness of God" (vv. 17 – 19). Likewise, they have been called to walk as one so that God might be glorified "in the church and in Christ Jesus throughout all generations" (v. 21).

In chapter 4, Paul intends to make known the administration of the mystery (Eph. 3:9), that is, to *demonstrate* for his readers how they can practically walk in a manner worthy of their calling to be one in Christ and in his church (Eph. 4:1). Given the diversity of the church and the inevitable conflicts that will arise, Paul instructs them to "be completely humble and gentle; be patient, bearing with one another in love. Make every effort to keep the unity of the Spirit through the bond of peace. There is one body and one Spirit — just as you were called to one hope when you were called — one Lord, one faith, one baptism; one God and Father of all, who is over all [of them] and [working] through all [of them] and [living] in [the midst of] all [of them]" (Eph. 4:2 – 6). Subsequently, he teaches them to work as one in regard to spiritual gifts and to walk together in truth, no longer according to their former (preconversion) ways of life (Eph. 4:7 – 5:20).

The theme of unity continues throughout chapter 5 as husbands are instructed to be one with their wives, and wives to be one with their husbands (5:21 – 33). In chapter 6, children are taught to be one with their parents, and parents to be one with their children (6:1 – 4). Slaves and masters (employees and employers) are also expected to walk and work in unity (6:5 – 9).

Again, throughout the whole of Ephesians, Paul's teaching is directed to individuals of various ethnicities, economic means, and generational statuses who collectively make up the local church at Ephesus.

"Finally," he writes in chapter 6, "be strong in the Lord and in his mighty power. Put on the full armor of God so that you can take your stand against the devil's schemes" (Eph. 6:10 – 11). This begs the question, Why does Paul place this significant teaching concerning the armor of God and spiritual warfare in this place and at this time in his letter? We should also ask, What is the struggle Paul has in mind as he is writing? Is it not a collective struggle to walk, work, and worship God together as one in and through the local church for the sake of the gospel?

Fortunately, we do not have to guess at the answer. For as Paul writes in conclusion, and to call attention to the spiritual forces of wickedness behind earthly divisions, "For our struggle is not against flesh and blood, but against the rulers, against the authorities, against the powers of this dark world and against the spiritual forces of evil in the heavenly realms" (Eph. 6:12).

All too often, we who have been born and raised in these doggedly independent United States fail to notice Paul's concern for unity, as well as the corporate dimension of spiritual attack, as we rush to render every "you" in this letter (and other letters of the New Testament) as singular! It is essential to recognize, however, that every "you" in this passage (Eph. 6:10 – 18) is plural, not singular. In other words, Paul's teaching concerning the spiritual struggle, one that requires *us* to put on the full armor of God, is focused not only on individual believers but also on the collective whole — namely, a gathered body of believers, the local church! Let's see how our understanding of this familiar passage changes as we emphasize the plural, corporate dimension of the word *you* through the following paraphrase of Ephesians 6:12 – 18:

> For your struggle as a church — to keep the unity of the Spirit in the bond of peace in spite of your diversity — is not rooted in differences related to the color of your skin (flesh) or diverse cultural backgrounds (blood); rather, it is a collective struggle against the rulers, authorities, and powers of this dark world and against the spiritual forces of evil in the heavenly realms. Therefore together as one, believing Jew and Gentile alike, you must put on the full armor of God so that when the day of evil comes, the church may be able to stand its ground, and after you have done everything, to stand in

unity together as one. Yes, stand firm together with the belt of truth buckled around your collective waist, with the breastplate of righteousness in place, and with your collective feet fitted with the readiness that comes from manifesting the gospel of peace to a lost and dying world. In addition to all this, take up the shield of faith, with which your church will be able to extinguish all the flaming arrows of the evil one which otherwise seek to divide and conquer. Yes, the church should put on the helmet of salvation and take up the sword of the Spirit, which is the word of God. And pray together as one in the Spirit on all occasions with all kinds of prayers and requests. With this in mind, be alert and always keep on praying together as one for all the saints in your church, no matter who they are or where they come from.

In view of the nature and inherent difficulty of promoting the multi-ethnic vision, is it any wonder that Paul goes on to ask for this church's prayers? But notice for what he asks them to pray: "that whenever I open my mouth,… I will fearlessly make known the mystery of the gospel, for which I am an ambassador in chains. Pray that I may declare it fearlessly, as I should" (Eph. 6:19 – 20). The reason why he is now a prisoner, Paul writes, is because he is making known the mystery of the gospel, the good news of Gentile inclusion as one with the Jews in Christ and in his church (Eph. 6:19 – 20; 3:3 – 6). Yes, as Acts 22 makes clear, it was not Paul's proclamation of Jesus as Messiah that irritated the Jews, but rather his message of Gentile inclusion in the kingdom of God. Indeed, it was only after he had spoken of Christ sending him to the Gentiles that the Jews assembled in the temple "raised their voices and shouted, 'Rid the earth of him! He's not fit to live!'" (Acts 22:21 – 22).

As we see, then, in Ephesians 6:10 – 18, Paul is not so much warning individual believers, "The Devil is out to get you!" Rather, he is warning the local church that the pursuit of unity is a collective struggle against unseen forces of darkness that will seek to separate us from one another and subvert the gospel's power, uniquely displayed when diverse believers walk, work, and worship God together as one. And looking back over the centuries of conflict and disunity in the church of Jesus Christ, I think it's safe to say that we have been losing one spiritual battle after another along the unity front! Petty struggles related to personal preference, past experience, and individual personality have long caused division upon division within the local church. In many cases, they have led to permanently damaged relationships among believers, congregational splits, unresolved doctrinal disputes, and a plethora of denominational division, all of which to this day continues to adversely affect the greater body of Christ and, more important, the credibility of the gospel of peace in the world.

Brothers and sisters, it should not be so!

BIZARRE BATTLES

As the apostle Paul alludes to in chapter 6 of his letter to the Ephesians, a unique level of spiritual warfare is inherent when you begin to pursue the vision of multi-ethnic ministry. Therefore, you should expect to be blindsided at times with bizarre and otherwise spiritually dark moments that can be attributed only to satanic schemes to take you out or keep you down. By way of example, here are just a few of the more "benign" stories we can share from our own experience at Mosaic.

Discouragement

A couple of years into our journey, I (Mark) encouraged a dear friend to remain at Mosaic and to pursue the restoration of his marriage in what I knew would be a safe and loving environment. For some time, he had involved himself with call girls while out of town on business. To his credit, he had now confessed this as sin and was ready to move beyond it all. Unfortunately, he was a little too eager to do so, seeking to spiritualize his experience in ways that downplayed the serious nature of his offense and the gravity of the situation.

When another pastor and I attempted to point this out in a meeting one day, with his best interests at heart, both this man

FIGHTING ON OUR KNEES: A SPIRITUAL CHALLENGE

David Anderson, Senior Pastor
Bridgeway Community Church, Columbia, Maryland

In the army, we were taught to stay together, watch each other's backs, and be on the lookout for the enemy, who works overtime to set up sneak attacks and ambushes. During our training exercises, my platoon would spend the night sleeping outside in the woods. When it was time to sleep, soldiers who were paired up would sleep in shifts. One soldier would sleep in the tent while the other remained awake to keep his eyes open for enemy combatants. It was imperative to trust that your partner would not fall asleep on the job while you were sleeping. After a couple of hours, we would trade places so that the one who was sleeping could keep watch while the other soldier could rest his tired eyes. We were taught that the enemy never sleeps.

The same is true about our spiritual enemy. Satan, the great deceiver and divider, works overtime to separate Christians, catch them while they are weak, worn, conflicted, confused, and, most of all, asleep. Just as Jesus' friends dozed off when they were supposed to stay awake and pray for him while he was facing the most difficult spiritual and emotional battle of his life in the garden of Gethsemane, we as believers have been lulled to sleep while the enemy prowls around like a roaring lion. As brothers and sisters in

Christ, we are called to watch each other's backs at all times, but especially in prayer. When we are careful to cover each other and stay unified against our common enemy, we find less time to argue and divide over our differences regarding race, ethnicity, denominational preferences, and the like.

When believers from every background begin to pray together, an undeniable unity emerges that elevates the spirit of oneness and diminishes the spirit of division. The enemy cannot fight effectively against a collection of believers who are more determined to "pray ... all kinds of prayers" (Eph 6:18) to fight against the principalities and spiritual forces of darkness that desire to stir up dissension and ethnic division.

Jesus prayed that his future disciples would be unified (John 17:20–21). Jesus didn't segregate his prayers either. He didn't pray that the white believers would be unified with their informational exegesis while black believers would be unified with their inspirational exposition. He didn't pray that Latinos would be unified in their praise while Asians would be unified in their practice. Jesus didn't pray that Jewish believers would be unified during Sabbath recognition on Friday evenings while Catholics would be uni-

cont.

fied during the Eucharist on Saturday nights. Jesus simply prayed that all the believers who came to believe in him would be one. Since this was the longest recorded prayer of Jesus in the Scriptures, isn't it fascinating that he passionately cried out for desegregated unity? How much more should we follow his example in our prayers and practice?

Those who pray for unity touch the heart of heaven as they seek to practice their faith across racial, ethnic, and denominational lines. When we pray together across such human boundaries, we are joining Jesus in praying, "Thy kingdom come, thy will be done on earth as it is in heaven." Jesus knew that the secret to real unity was prayer, all kinds of prayers. Multicultural, multi-ethnic, and multi-generational prayer is the single most effective weapon against the enemy who seeks to separate and divide. Many talk a good game about racial unity. But the real question is, Are we willing to fight for racial unity on our knees?

and his wife suddenly turned on me as if I were the enemy! In an almost trancelike state, they thrust their right arms in my direction, bowed their heads together, closed their eyes, and screamed in unison such things as, "Get behind me, Satan!... I command you, do not speak!... Forgive him, Lord!... Help us, Jesus!" I was shocked at the look my friend was giving me, like the cold stare of a shark — penetrating, piercing my eyes as if to inflict a wound. I had known this man for many years, yet in that moment I knew there was something truly demonic about his gaze.

By the end of the meeting, the other pastor and I were able to regain control of the situation and calmly close with this couple in prayer. Yet following our time together with them, the two of us talked and agreed: we had come face-to-face that afternoon with forces of darkness out to destroy us all individually, as well as our fledgling church. Soon this couple too would leave the church and, as in the case of Shelly's departure, cause a wave of confusion, doubt, and distrust among our membership.

For me personally, it was all so discouraging at the time, especially in light of who was involved, a dear friend. In those days, I remember agreeing with David: "If an enemy were insulting me,

I could endure it; if a foe were raising himself against me, I could hide from him. But it is you, a man like myself, my companion, my close friend, with whom I once enjoyed sweet fellowship as we walked with the throng at the house of God" (Ps. 55:12 – 14).

So how do you deal with such discouragement, the wounds of a friend? Though hurt may linger and feelings take time to recover, "cast your cares on the LORD and he will sustain you; [be assured] he will never let the righteous fall" (Ps. 55:22).

Disruption

One Sunday, we decided to replace the sermon with an extended time of prayer. Having positioned several microphones through-out the worship area, we began the service that day by asking people to read Scripture, so as to pray over the body. Not long after we began, I (Harry) remember thinking that the presence of the Lord was evident and working in a very powerful way. Just then, a homeless man who frequents the church stood up and shouted, "The Word of God says, 'Resist the Devil and he will flee from you.' So I'm fleeing!" Turning swiftly, he then ran frantically out of the service, exorcising himself right out of the building!

Fortunately, we went on to enjoy a powerful time of worship.

Danger

On another occasion, a man came into the building asking for help. Together with Mike Clowers, our executive pastor, I (Harry) sat down with him, and soon a very serious discussion about his life ensued. Through tears, the man prayed in all sincerity to accept Jesus into his life. Following this spiritual interaction, Mike took him back into our food and clothing distribution cen-ter, located in a rather remote part of the church. The man was very thankful to receive the assistance and left us in good spirits, promising to return.

Two weeks later, however, we saw this same man's face plastered all over the news; he had just been arrested for having committed twelve armed robberies in the Little Rock area, hitting several banks and a toy store. In fact, he had posed for his mug shot in a hoodie we had given him! As we put the pieces together, we suddenly recognized the timing of his visit to Mosaic. It was right in the middle of his crime spree that he had come to us for help, probably seeking to "steal ... and destroy" (John 10:10). Looking back, we believe that the Holy Spirit somehow convicted the man through our authentic demonstration of peace and love, keeping us from harm or loss.

Distraction

There's a woman who has been visiting our church on and off for several years. Sometimes homeless and always erratic, she can be quite distracting. In fact, she has been known to yell out racial slurs while telling others how much she hates them. One Sunday morning, this woman came into our service, walked up to the front, and flashed our worship leader, lifting her shirt to bare it all. Take it from us, it was nothing you'd want to see! And bless his heart, Cesar Ortega remained surprisingly calm in the face of the distraction. In fact, he didn't miss a beat. We all knew that the woman was mentally unstable, but make no mistake: her actions intentionally challenged the very message of our church, in much the same way as did the actions of the confused woman in Acts 16, who was giving Paul fits (Acts 16:16 – 18).

You can expect similar distractions as you balance the tension between patience and prudence in extending the love of God to all people, and especially in extending his love to "the least of these," both in and outside the church.

PERSONAL ATTACKS

Personal attacks are common enough in ministry. But in a church with an intentional vision for unity, the frequency and fervency of personal hits, hurts, and hindrances are greatly enhanced. I (Mark) believe that all of this is intended by spiritual forces to distract, discourage, and outright destroy our families and churches and, of course, those of us bold enough to lead them.

In fact, I have a confession to make. As I sit here writing this chapter, I am under the most intense spiritual attack I have experienced in more than twenty-five years of full-time ministry. It is one I have been battling for approximately three months. And the forces of darkness have hit deeply and personally this time.

I think this particular battle is so powerful because it is strongly rooted in my past. More specifically, I am grieving certain losses experienced more than thirty years ago. These are relational losses that I cannot go back to repair or recover, the emotions of which, I now realize, have been compartmentalized to this point.

Graciously, God has provided a dear friend from college who listened to my pains and concerns without judging, guided without demanding, and prayed without ceasing when I first became disoriented. At that time, I also shared generally of my struggle with friends and colleagues with whom I am associated in a Learning Community through Leadership Network. In that moment, I so greatly appreciated the leadership of Dave Travis and Linda Stanley, who, upon learning of my grief, quickly organized a monthlong daily prayer vigil. And I know now that the prayers of the people in that group sustained me in those early, very difficult days.

One month later I also shared of my struggle with another spiritual leader in Phoenix, Arizona. And just yesterday I contacted another friend for further counseling. Ironically, a pastor called today from Chicago, and I felt safe, as well, to speak about it with him. Like all the rest, he too prayed for me, provided good guidance, and offered the promise of continued encouragement until God helps me through to the other side.

Most important, my wife, Linda, is now aware of my struggle with grief. With extreme grace and kindness, Linda has determined to love me through it. In her so doing, I have been reminded again that she is an amazing woman of Christ-centered faith and character. She is truly a gift beyond what I otherwise deserve.

All this is to say that such people are now helping me to overcome this attack and to come out the stronger for it in Christ. In discussing it at this time, I hope not only to reinforce the theme of this chapter but also to encourage you with two other thoughts.

First, if you are similarly struggling with a personal attack, a potentially destructive secret, or an area of outright sin, I strongly encourage you to find a person (or people) in whom you can confide. Indeed, do not deny your pain or try to cover it up — you can do significant damage to yourself, your family, and your church by attempting to hide the truth.

Second, recognize that to struggle with something is not necessarily to sin. I often grow tired of unrealistic expectations that deny our humanity as pastors and spiritual leaders. In other words, we who have been led to lead others spiritually are not perfect, just people pursuing what we believe to be God's will for our lives.[4] The fact is, God knows both our hearts and our weaknesses when he calls us to serve him by serving others. Therefore I do not pastor or preach because I'm perfect; I pastor and preach because I have been called by God to do so to the best of my ability, in authenticity and integrity. And for twenty-eight years that is what I've done.

Therefore remember that God is not surprised when pains, weaknesses, and deficiencies rear their ugly head in our lives. The real question is, How will we handle our struggles? Where will we go with our pain and our failure? Will we run to God or run away from him?

Let me remind you how deep and unfailing the Father's love is for all who are his children. Even when we fail him, we should never doubt his love. Ain't nothing can take that away! That said, I in no way want to suggest that any one of us should use the certainty of God's forgiveness to indulge the sinful nature (Gal. 5:13). For while "everything is permissible for me ... not everything is beneficial" (1 Cor. 6:12). When we learn to rely upon the Lord and trust in the hope of the gospel each day, we grow in our understanding of God's grace, patiently and compassionately dealing with others when they struggle and sin. As we openly confess our sin and rely upon God's righteousness and not our own, we will grow in humility while we lead others and express greater dependence upon God from day to day. This is a much more realistic goal for pastors than striving to be perfect before people.

YOU ARE NOT ALONE

As we have shared throughout this chapter, local church pastors and planters can expect to face unique and various forms of spiritual assault as they pursue ethnic blends. In spite of this, we can and must stay the course, guided by a most powerful truth: "the one who is in you is greater than the one who is in the world" (1 John 4:4).

One afternoon in the early days of Mosaic, I was at a local gas station just up the street from the building where we were gathering as a church on Sundays. After filling the tank, I had gone inside to pay. While standing in line, I noticed that the female clerk had a Korean Bible open and lying on the counter. The pages I could see were marked with various colored highlighters, and I could tell she had been studying. When at last it was my turn to be waited upon, I struck up a brief conversation, informing her about our new church plant, its location in the neighborhood, and our heart for bringing diverse people together — hoping she would be interested and possibly attend a service. Stepping aside for the last person in line, I continued talking to her while she completed the man's transaction. At that particular moment, I was speaking of the need for multiethnic churches through which believers might learn to love one another in Christ, and the subsequent impact such churches would have on society. Finishing his business, the man at the counter turned and headed for the door. On his way out, clearly intending to be heard, he commented, "Boy, I need to get me some boots; it's getting thick in here!"

As you read those words, I can imagine you're thinking, "No big deal," right? Just let it go. But the tone and tenor of the man's comment was clearly racist. There was no doubt in my mind — and from the look on the Korean woman's face, I could tell there was no doubt in hers — that the man's comment was intended to offend. So in an instant I reacted foolishly and followed the man outside. Walking briskly, I caught up to him as he approached his car, and asked, "Excuse me, sir. What did you just say?"

As I reflect on the incident, I am thankful that this man did not turn to confront me! I can just imagine the headlines if there had been an altercation: "Local Church Pastor Seeking to Love All People Today Kicked the Butt of a Good Ol' White Boy Racist!"

Instead the man rudely and loudly replied, "You know what I mean … We don't need your kind here!" And it was that statement that stopped me dead in my tracks.

By then the Korean clerk was running out the door, waving her arms and shouting in broken English, "No trouble please! No trouble here!" It was quite the scene.

As he drove away, several thoughts crossed my mind. First, it dawned on me that I could have been killed. I was in a neighborhood boasting the highest violent crime rate in the state, and that man could have easily pulled a gun on me. Second, it saddened me to realize that it was now highly unlikely that this Korean woman would ever set foot in our church. And finally, I thought, "Oh my gosh, I've just been racially and spiritually slandered!" — something which, to my knowledge, I had never experienced before. It was a moment that gave me new perspective and an increased empathy for many minorities who in one way or another are forced to endure such things on a daily basis.

Over the years, Harry and I have seen people leave our church, misrepresent our character, and alter the facts of a situation in an effort to sow doubt or discord within our church body. Often, those who attack us know that we will not speak up to defend ourselves, and at times they have sought to use that against us. Some have even tried to draw others away in the process. And we once had to deal with another church that was specifically targeting some of our more influential members, without talking to us first, and pressuring them to leave Mosaic.

GOD WINS AGAIN!

David Boyd, Senior Pastor
Jesus Family Centre, Sydney, Australia

From the very beginning of our church plant in an economically depressed suburb of Sydney, we experienced spiritual challenges that could be attributed only to "the powers of this dark world and ... spiritual forces of evil in the heavenly realms" (Eph. 6:12). For example, I can vividly remember attempting to pray with my wife, Chih Yunn, and the team on numerous occasions, after we had put our children to bed. Inevitably, just as we would begin to pray against the demonic atmosphere in the area, one of our children would begin to cry hysterically! While children waking up crying may not be an uncommon experience for parents of small children, the coincidence of this happening only when we focused on this subject, and the fervency of our children's cries, led us in time to recognize that there was something more behind it all: darkness, distraction, demonic forces aligned against us and against a church that would dare to call diverse people to worship God as one. It was a demonic oppression that would take many years to break through the power of faith, obedience, and prayer.

In those days, Cabramatta was the location of hostels, where refugees would be placed upon arrival in Australia. They would be given three months of orientation before they were required to find their own accommodations. They arrived by the tens of thousands, bringing their own worldviews, values, and gods with them. In time, many of these people settled in the surrounding area, contributing greatly to Cabramatta's diversity of beliefs and cultures. Today Cabramatta is located in a region believed to be one of the most diverse in the world.

Many of the Christians who came to us in those early days came with a mindset to "help us" but not necessarily with a calling to "join us" in the work. One man from Malaysia illustrates this attitude. Initially, he came with his family to reach the growing Chinese community around us, an area that boasted 40 percent of all the Chinese people living in Sydney at the time. After becoming integrated in the church, however, the man felt he was not receiving adequate remuneration for his efforts; at that time the church was unable to pay more so could not meet his expectations. Eventually he began to complain to others in the body, causing dissension. The confusion he sowed soon led to a church split: 50 percent of the people who were with us at the time simply walked away.

Through that experience, however, I learned two significant lessons about overcoming these spiritual obstacles.

First, it is important to stay focused on your goal of establishing

cont.

a multi-ethnic church and not to let distractions, whether demonic or human in origin, knock you off course. Second, I learned not to try to keep people from leaving when they choose to flee when the going gets tough. By applying these two principles in those days, we not only weathered the storm but also came out the other side the better for it.

Ultimately, God brought good from this difficult season of our ministry. At the time, it forced people to choose not simply to help but to fully commit themselves to us, to one another, and to the vision. Consequently, a more committed leadership team emerged from the ashes, one that has largely remained intact for nearly fourteen years. Through the years, we have developed a oneness in Christ and in the church, embraced a common vision and purpose, and brought stability to the work, enabling health and growth.

Today approximately forty nations and ninety different ethnic groups are represented in the four hundred attendees on a Sunday morning. In addition, the church has planted nearly thirty churches in seven countries outside Australia, and each one is passionately committed to reflecting the heart of God for all people in its membership and its outreach. God wins again!

Of course, local church pastors and planters everywhere will identify with us in these matters and surely can recall their own similar stories of spiritual persecution. Indeed, every church will likely face similar challenges. But in a multi-ethnic church, where race and class issues are also in play, the frustrations tend to be exponentially magnified. We often recognize the broader significance of what's at stake. Our failure to keep the unity of the Spirit through the bond of peace — the very purpose and stated intent of the church — will threaten the fragile confidence of those both in and outside the church who still wonder if the dream can really be achieved.

Instead of allowing yourself to get discouraged, stay focused on God and allow his Spirit to fire you up time and time again. Remember that those who pursue the path of the peacemaker, investing their lives in multi-ethnic ministry, are following in the very footsteps of Christ and the apostle Paul. Take to heart the words of Paul as he reflected on his own work of planting and developing multi-ethnic churches. He wrote to Timothy, "You, however, know all about my teaching, my way of life, my purpose, faith, patience, love, endurance, persecutions, sufferings — what kinds of things happened to me in Antioch, Iconium and Lystra, the persecutions I endured. Yet the Lord rescued me from all of them. In fact, everyone who wants to live a godly life in Christ Jesus will be persecuted" (2 Tim. 3:10 – 12).

Be encouraged, then, and know that you are not alone in facing these spiritual challenges. The obstacles can be overcome as the Lord is with you. In his time, through his grace, he will rescue you from them all. Indeed, "the one who calls you is faithful and he will do it" (1 Thess. 5:24)!

QUESTIONS FOR REFLECTION AND DISCUSSION

1. Can you describe a time in your life or ministry when the bizarre behavior of someone else toward you led you to believe that spiritual forces of wickedness were involved in trying to discourage you personally, undermine your efforts, or otherwise sabotage your work? What was at stake? What lingering concerns, fears, or attitudes do you still carry from the attack?

2. Have you ever considered Christ's teaching concerning peacemakers, both the good of identification with him as a son of God and the bad of persecution that quite naturally goes with the territory? When it comes to pursuit of the multi-ethnic church, are you up to the challenge?

3. Review and discuss the teaching in this chapter concerning spiritual warfare as described by Paul in Ephesians 6. Have you ever associated this very familiar passage concerning the armor of God with what is necessary for the church to put on in order to walk worthy of its calling to be one for the sake of

the gospel? Have you before recognized that the struggle Paul is talking about is the struggle for a church to walk in a manner worthy of its calling to be one (Eph. 4:1)? How do such considerations enlighten or confuse your understanding of the biblical mandate for the multi-ethnic church?

4. Are you currently struggling with a personal spiritual attack, a potentially destructive secret, or an area of outright sin? Take a moment to consider its root cause. In other words, what has led you to this place and why? Who can you call confidentially to seek understanding, encouragement, help, counsel, or accountability? Will you do it for your own sake, the sake of your spouse, the sake of your children, the sake of your ministry? What's stopping you from placing a call to that person right now?

5. What key thought, revelation, or insight will you take away from this chapter? What is God asking you to do in response?

AN EVERLASTING AROMA
Conclusion

> There before me was a great multitude that no one could
> count, from every nation, tribe, people and language, stand-
> ing before the throne and in front of the Lamb.... And they
> cried out in [one] loud voice: "Salvation belongs to our God."
> — *Revelation 7:9 – 10*

FOR THE PAST TWENTY-TWO YEARS, my good friend Mathew Kuru-
villa has served as the senior pastor of Parkside Baptist Church
in Edensor Park, a suburb of Sydney, Australia. Born and raised
in India, he has been living in Australia since 1976. His church
is located next door to a Buddhist temple and behind a Moslem
mosque, reflecting a demographic future that many people living
in the United States still cannot envision. Yet under his leadership,
Parkside has successfully transitioned from a homogeneous church
to a multi-ethnic one by taking intentional steps.

When Mathew became the pastor at Parkside, for instance, he
recognized that the church did not reflect the community. Convinced of the multi-ethnic nature of the New Testament church and
its purpose, he first developed a sermon series in order to enlighten
his congregation on the subject. By beginning with Scripture,
Mathew sought to align the people with God's vision for the local
church. Once they understood this vision, he believed, they would
pursue it with passion.

Second, Mathew led his people to pray for the community on a
consistent basis. On Sunday mornings, Wednesday nights, and even
on Saturdays, he invited his congregation to gather with him specifically for that purpose. These times provided additional opportunities for Mathew to educate his people about the community, about
the people living within it and their specific needs. In addition, he
explained to his people that in order to reach the community for
Christ, the church would have to change.

Before his arrival, the church believed that the Great Commission (Matt. 28:19–20) was something to be lived out by missionaries around the world. Because of Mathew's efforts, however, the people of Parkside soon realized that the Great Commission was something they were to live out across the street as well. Initially, just one couple embraced the vision. In time, however, others followed, and soon the whole church was committed not only to reaching the community *outside* its doors but also to reflecting the community *within* its doors, for the sake of the gospel.

A final step was taken when the church redefined its vision by adopting a new mission statement that is still operative today. It reads, "Parkside is a Christian community committed to bring Christ to people of all nations in our community."

Given the successful transformation — that is, in becoming a multi-ethnic church — Parkside today reflects a united, diverse congregation of evangelical faith. But as Mathew shares, the church is not as focused as it once was on the ethnic diversity of its people; rather, it's now focused on the eternal destiny of people they seek to influence through their collective witness. Thus, Mathew has brought the church full circle, and I believe its journey forecasts the future for us as well.

You see, someday, I believe, multi-ethnic churches will be largely assumed and accepted by Christ-centered people everywhere — or as David Olson has written, they will become "the normal and natural face of Christianity."[1] In that day, the church of the twenty-first century will reflect the church of the first century; it will be one in which diverse men and women quite naturally walk, work, and worship God together as one for the sake of the gospel. When that happens, there may no longer be a need to emphasize ethnicity within the local church as this book has done, but I'm so fine with that! Then, finally, the local church will truly reflect the heart of God for all people on earth as it is in heaven. It will be able to proclaim Christ as Savior with credibility in a diverse and cynical society. His prayer will have been answered, and the world will come to know Jesus as we do. Indeed, in that day God's house will be called a house of prayer for *all the nations*, and together with *all the saints*, we will enjoy with our Father the everlasting aroma of ethnic blends.

Appendix 1

CHURCH PROFILES

THE FOLLOWING INFORMATION was self-reported in April 2009 by pastors and ministry leaders contributing to the book. In some cases, statistical and demographic information reflects a good-faith estimate at the time of their writing. The churches are listed here in order of their appearance within these pages.

"HOLY DISCONTENT" (P. 65)
Wayne Schmidt (Anglo American)
Senior Pastor
Kentwood Community Church
Kentwood, Michigan
www.kentwoodcommunitychurch.com
Weekend attendance: 2,700
White (87%), Black (11%), Hispanic/Latino and Asian (2%)

"IN HIS WAY AND TIME" (P. 69)
Michael S. Leonzo (Anglo American)
Lead Pastor
Living Water Community Church
Harrisburg, Pennsylvania
www.livingwatercc.com
Weekend attendance: 500
White (80%), African American (10%), Hispanic/Latino (5%), Other (5%)

"JUST DO IT" (P. 82)
David Nelms (Anglo American)
Lead Pastor
Grace Fellowship
West Palm Beach, Florida
www.GFWPB.org
Weekend attendance: 3,089
White (35%), Jamaican (25%), Haitian (20%), Hispanic/Latino (10%),
    Asian (5%), Multi-ethnic/Other (5%)

"UNSHAKABLE CONVICTION" (P. 95)

Jonathan P. Seda (Hispanic American)
Senior Pastor
Grace Church
Dover, Delaware
www.gracedover.com
Weekend attendance: 350
White (82%), Black (7%), Hispanic/Latino (8%), Multi-ethnic/
Other (3%)

"MORE THAN MERE TOOLS" (P. 104)

Alejandro (Alex) Mandes (Hispanic American)
Director of Hispanic Ministries and Gateway
Evangelical Free Church of America
Minneapolis, Minnesota

"PURSUING THE DREAM" (P. 119)

Edward M. Lee (Chinese American)
Lead Pastor
Mosaic Community Covenant Church
Sugar Land, Texas
www.mosaicpeople.org
Weekend attendance: 72
Asian (44%), White (19%), Multi-ethnic/Other (16%), African
American (15%), Hispanic/Latino (6%)

"ECLECTIC WORSHIP" (P. 135)

Daniel Backens (Anglo American)
Senior Pastor
New Life Providence Church
Chesapeake, Virginia
www.newlifeprovidence.com
Weekend attendance: 2,100
White (50%), African American (40%), Hispanic/Latino (5%), Multi-
ethnic/Other (3%), Asian (2%)

"CREATING THE SWIRL" (P. 142)

Chris Williamson (African American)

Senior Pastor
Strong Tower Bible Church
Franklin, Tennessee
www.strongtowerbiblechurch.com
Weekend attendance: 750
African American (44%), White (43%), Other, including Native American, Hispanic/Latino, Asian, and African (13%)

"CONNECTION AND COMMUNITY" (P. 155)

Dana Baker (Anglo American)
Director of Multicultural Ministries
Grace Chapel
Lexington, Massachusetts
www.grace.org
Weekend attendance: 3,000
White (70%), Asian/Pacific Islander (20%), African American, African, and Caribbean (4%), Hispanic/Latino (4%), Multi-ethnic/Other (2%)

"INCLUSIVE THINKING" (P. 164)

Mont Mitchell (Anglo American)
Senior Pastor
Westbrook Christian Church
Bolingbrook, Illinois
www.westbrookchurch.org
Weekend attendance: 1,200
White (55%), Hispanic/Latino (20%), African American (15%), Pan Asian (10%)

"THE ELEPHANT IN THE ROOM" (P. 179)

Efrem Smith (African American)
Senior Pastor
Sanctuary Covenant Church
Minneapolis, Minnesota
www.sanctuarycovenant.org
Weekend attendance: 1,100
White (50%), African American (40%), Asian and Hispanic/Latino (10%)

"EMOTIONAL HEALTH" (P. 186)

Peter Scazzero (Anglo American)
Senior/Lead Pastor
New Life Fellowship Church
Queens, New York City
www.newlifefellowship.org, www.emotionallyhealthy.org
Weekend attendance: 1,100
Hispanic/Latino (25%), Asian American (25%), African American
   (20%), White (15%), Eastern European (10%), Other (5%)

"FIGHTING ON OUR KNEES" (P. 201)

David Anderson (African American)
Senior Pastor
Bridgeway Community Church
Columbia, Maryland
www.bridgewayonline.org
Weekend attendance: 2,425
African American (56%), White (24%), African (6%), Asian (6%), Multi-
   ethnic/Other (5%), Hispanic/Latino (2%), Native American (1%)

"GOD WINS AGAIN!" (P. 209)

David Boyd (Scottish)
Senior Pastor
Jesus Family Centre
Sydney, Australia
www.newlifeintl.net
Weekend attendance: 400
Asian (70%), African (15%), White (10%), Hispanic/Latino and Other (5%)

Appendix 2

MOSAIX

Catalyzing the Movement toward Multi-ethnic Churches throughout North America and Beyond!

MISSION

To enlist, equip, and establish local church leaders who desire to develop multi-ethnic congregations of Christ-centered faith for the sake of the gospel.

VISION

To see 20 percent of local churches in the United States achieve a minimum of 20 percent diversity in their attendance/membership by the year 2020, and beyond that, to see 50 percent of local churches in the United States achieve 50 percent diversity by the year 2050.

DEVELOPMENTAL STRATEGY

To inspire unity and diversity in the local church by (1) casting vision, (2) connecting individuals of like mind, (3) conferencing, and (4) coaching.

For more information or to get involved, contact
www.mosaix.info

OF GIFTS AND LOVE

Comparing Paul's Thoughts in 1 Corinthians 12 – 14 with Those in Ephesians 4

UNITY OF THE BODY

1 Corinthians 12:12 – 27

> One Spirit, one body, whether Jews or Greeks (v. 13).
>
> There should be no division in the body (v. 25).
>
> The parts (of the body) should have equal concern for each other (v. 25).

Ephesians 4:3 – 6, 16

> Make every effort to keep the unity of the Spirit (v. 3).
>
> There is one body and one Spirit (v. 4).
>
> The whole body is joined and held together by every supporting ligament (v. 16).

GIFTS IN THE BODY

1 Corinthians 12:28 – 30

> Apostles, prophets, teachers … healing, helps, administration, etc. (12:28).

Ephesians 4:7, 11 – 13

> Apostles, prophets, evangelists, pastors, and teachers (v. 11).

CORRECTION OF THE BODY

1 Corinthians 12:31 – 14:40

> In your immaturity, you are seeking showy gifts. Mature as one in love! (12:25, 29 – 31).

Ephesians 4:14 – 16

> No prolonged infancies among us, please. Mature as one in love (vv. 14 – 16).

LOVE IN THE BODY

1 Corinthians 13

> If I speak ... but have not love ... (v. 1).

> Love is patient, love is kind.... It is not rude, not self seeking (vv. 4 – 5).

Ephesians 4:2, 15 – 16

> Speaking the truth in love (v. 15).

> Be patient, bearing with one another in love (v. 2).

BUILDING UP THE BODY

1 Corinthians 14:4 – 5, 12, 17, 19

> To edify, build up the church (vv. 4 – 5, 12).

Ephesians 4:12

> So that the body of Christ may be built up (v. 12).

MATURITY IN THE BODY

1 Corinthians 14:20

> Brothers, stop thinking like children (v. 20).

Ephesians 4:13 – 14

> Until we all ... become mature, ... then we will no longer be infants (vv. 13 – 14).

Appendix 4

VARIATIONS OF
MULTI-ETHNIC CHURCHES

ED LEE, pastor of the Mosaic Community Covenant Church in Sugar Land, Texas, first developed this chart for presentation as part of the Multi-ethnic Track (presented by the Mosaix Global Network) at the National New Church Conference (Exponential) in Orlando, Florida (2008). Subsequent interaction with me (Mark), Dr. Willie Peterson, Mont Mitchell, and others brought some refinement, whereby experienced practitioners and researchers alike now all agree that it is a valuable tool for those seeking to build a healthy multi-ethnic church. My thanks to Ed for allowing us the privilege to call attention to his work and publish it here in *Ethnic Blends*.

VARIATIONS OF MULTI-ETHNIC CHURCHES BY THE REVEREND ED LEE

Nuance	Biblical Mandate				
	Variation 1	Variation 2	Variation 3	Variation 4	Variation 5
Emphasis	1.0 outreach	world missions	local evangelism	racial reconciliation	community engagement
Core Commitment	empower diverse leadership	mobilize for impact	develop cross-cultural competence	take intentional steps	develop cross-cultural relationships
Culture	distinguishes cultures	celebrates culture	respects culture	creates "one new" culture	reaches subculture
Strategic Development	establishing ethnic churches through ethnic pastors	mobilizing diverse members to reach their nation	encouraging diverse people to walk together as one	addressing the lingering impact of systemic racism	mobilizing members to be culturally relevant
Motivation	to fulfill the Great Commission locally	to fulfill the Great Commission worldwide	to reflect God's kingdom here on earth	to provide an answer to the problem of race	to reach those disaffected by church
Worship	separate services for separate congregations	inclusive multicultural elements in worship	accommodates different styles	varied worship based on the worship leader	includes the arts beyond music
Leadership	majority over minority	majority adds minority	diverse leadership	shared power	community partners
Generational Impact	helping first-generation immigrants	reaching first-generation immigrants w/English	reaching first and second generations	targeting second and third generations	targeting the emerging, blended generations
Language	separate-language congregation	English w/multiple languages in worship	English w/simultaneous translation	English only	English only
Biblical Basis	Matt. 28:19–20 "disciples of all nations"	Acts 1:8 "to the ends of the earth"	John 17:20–23 "one to make him known"	Eph. 2:14–16 "one new man"	Matt. 25:35–39 "you clothed me"
Cautions	may be too separate	may be too global-minded	may be too idealistic	may be too unrealistic	may be too self-serving
Outcomes	1.0 leadership is empowered	the world is evangelized	vibrant community is experienced	reconciliation is encountered	the wandering soul is enlightened

Variations are listed in no particular order of importance.

Appendix 5

CONFLICT NORMS FOR PASTORAL STAFF AND ELDERS

Mosaic Church of Central Arkansas

IN A MINISTRY WHERE DIVERSE INDIVIDUALS are seeking to discern God's leading and direction for themselves and others, it will not be unusual to find differing opinions or for individuals to hold various views on matters pertaining to life and the church. In the interest of unity, and while engaging in honest discussion, it is essential to the overall health of our body and our leadership team that we understand and embrace the following conflict norms — or ground rules — to govern our working relationships.

With this in mind, let us commit ourselves to these principles of behavior:

1. We will remember that we are on the same team, fighting for the same cause (Eph. 4:3; Rom. 15:1 – 6; Phil. 2:1 – 2).
2. We will believe the best about one another (Phil. 4:8; 1 Cor. 13).
3. We will listen well to one another (Prov. 19:20; Jer. 17:23).
4. We will avoid gossip and a critical spirit and not take disagreement or differences personally (Rom. 1:29; 2 Cor. 12:20; 1 Tim. 5:13).
5. We will engage in healthy dialogue, disagreements, and conflict with one another (Prov. 1:5; 2:2 – 3; 1 John 3:18).
6. We will point out unresolved conflict to one another (Matt. 18:15 – 35).
7. We will accept our personal responsibility to resolve conflict in a biblical manner (Matt. 18:15 – 35).

8. We will resolve conflict in the proper setting and timing (Matt. 18:15 – 35).

9. We will acknowledge issues and address the obvious (Eph. 4:15).

10. We will be honest and not retreat (Prov. 27:6).

NOTES

INTRODUCTION

1. See Curtiss Paul DeYoung, Michael O. Emerson, George Yancey, and Karen Chai Kim, *United by Faith: The Multiracial Congregation as an Answer to the Problem of Race* (New York: Oxford Univ. Press, 2003). The authors cite Mark Chavez, "National Congregations Study" (Tucson, Ariz.: Univ. of Arizona Department of Sociology, 1999).

2. My good friend D. J. Chuang consistently provides the most up-to-date bibliography on his website. Visit *www.djchuang.com/multi/* (April 29, 2009) for the most current and composite list.

3. To learn more, visit *www.thenewculture.org* (April 30, 2009).

4. To learn more, visit *www.exponentialconference.org* (April 30, 2009).

5. To learn more, visit *www.ethnic-america.net* (April 30, 2009).

6. The Mosaix Global Network, founded by Mark DeYmaz and George Yancey, was a five-year pioneering effort (2004 – 2009) that successfully established a relational network for likeminded pastors, church planters, researchers, and educators pursuing the multi-ethnic vision. Today, the Mosaix carries on this work. Visit www.mosaix.info to learn more.

CHAPTER I: I'LL DRINK TO THAT!

1. David Olson, *The American Church in Crisis* (Grand Rapids, Mich.: Zondervan, 2008), 170 – 71.

2. The term majority-minority is used to describe a U.S. state or other jurisdiction whose racial composition is less than 50 percent white. See Conor Dougherty, "Whites to Lose Majority Status in U.S. by 2042," Wall Street Journal, August 14, 2008, A3, *http://online.wsj.com/article/SB121867492705539109.html* (accessed September 23, 2009).

3. George Yancey, *One Body, One Spirit* (Downers Grove, Ill.: InterVarsity Press, 2005).

4. More information is available from *www.mosaix.info* (August 2009).

5. *Encarta World English Dictionary*, 1999.

6. Ibid.
7. Available from *www.duke.edu/web/equity/cultural_competency
.pdf* (February 5, 2007).
8. Spencer Perkins and Chris Rice, *More Than Equals* (Downers
Grove, Ill.: InterVarsity Press, 2000), 261.

CHAPTER 2: BLENDING AS A FAMILY

1. Darryl DelHousaye is currently (April 2009) the president of
Phoenix Seminary in Phoenix, Arizona.
2. Little Rock's Central High School was forcibly integrated in 1957,
following Brown v. Board of Education (1954), and the school's
integration endures as a major milestone of the American civil
rights movement. More information is available from *www.nps
.gov/chsc* (February 20, 2009).
3. Keep in mind, these verses were written to and within the
context of a multi-ethnic church.
4. These concepts are fully developed in *Building a Healthy Multi-
ethnic Church* (San Francisco: Jossey-Bass/Leadership Network,
2007), chaps. 1 – 3.

CHAPTER 3: HARVESTING TIPS
FROM THE OLD COUNTRY

1. On a side note, to this day we still approach the communion
table in this manner twice each month. Perhaps because of my
Catholic roots, I like the symbolism of people coming forward as
if to the cross, as opposed to sitting back waiting for God again
to come to them.
2. Exegesis of this portion of the Greek text was provided by Dr.
Greg Kappas and built on a previous study of the passage by
Dr. Earl Radmacher. See also *Nelson's New Illustrated Bible
Commentary* (Nashville: Nelson, 1999), 1481.
3. See appendix 3 for a comparative chart of the amazing
similarities of these two passages.
4. Our doctrinal statement and some position papers can be found
at our website, *www.mosaicchurch.net.*
5. To learn more about the Duke Center for Reconciliation, visit
http://www.divinity.duke.edu/reconciliation/index.html (accessed
November 6, 2009).

6. See Chris Rice, "Credibility for Christianity: A Revival at America's Margins," posted October 25, 2009 at *http://reconcilers.wordpress.com*.

7. Interaction via email with Chris Rice, November 10, 2009.

CHAPTER 4: REGULAR OR DECAF?

1. To read our position paper on the subject of politics, go to *www.mosaicchurch.net*.

2. In fact, instances of multi-ethnic churches at the beginning of the twenty-first century were even lower than what should otherwise have been expected, according to the findings of Michael Emerson and Christian Smith, as reported in their groundbreaking work *Divided by Faith* (Oxford: Oxford Univ. Press, 2001), 122ff.

3. The story of our first attempt at integration is taken from Mark DeYmaz, *Building a Healthy Multi-ethnic Church* (San Francisco: Jossey-Bass/Leadership Network, 2007), 55.

4. Prior to this, our 1.0 Hispanics could meet as part of the church for discipleship, for tutoring, or for special occasions, etc., but only off-site — in homes, for example, or otherwise away from our facility. I should also note that from the beginning, we have sponsored a youth group for students attending the local Deaf School.

5. Dr. Bird's article was published on July 15, 2008, under "The Question of the Week" at *Learnings @ Leadership Network*: *http://learnings.leadnet.org/2008/07/index.html* (April 6, 2009).

6. Geoff Surratt, *Ten Stupid Things That Keep Churches from Growing* (Grand Rapids, Mich.: Zondervan, 2009).

CHAPTER 5: CAN I POUR YOU A CUP?

1. The word *teteleiomenoi* (perfect passive plural) is so translated at *www.greekbible.com/index.php* (April 6, 2009).

2. For more on the continuum of unity, including a more detailed graphic, see Mark DeYmaz, *Building a Healthy Multi-ethnic Church* (San Francisco: Jossey-Bass/Leadership Network, 2007), 180–81.

3. According to research conducted by sociologists Curtiss Paul DeYoung, Michael O. Emerson, George Yancey, and Karen Chai Kim, 92.5 percent of Catholic and Protestant churches

throughout the United States can be classified as "mono-racial." This term describes a church in which 80 percent or more of the individuals who attend are of the same ethnicity or race. The remaining churches (7.5 percent) can be described as multiracial churches, in which there is a nonmajority, collective population of at least 20 percent. By this definition, approximately 12 percent of Catholic churches, just less than 5 percent of evangelical churches, and about 2.5 percent of mainline Protestant churches can be described as multiracial.

4. For more as to why you should and how you can effectively reconfigure the self-centered mindsets of people attempting to impose their own preferences for music upon the whole, see *Building a Healthy Multi-ethnic Church*, chap. 9.

5. This quote was taken from an online article at *www.guitarnoise .com/lesson/pentatonic-blues-origins/* and adapted from a course developed by Rick Payne titled "Pentatonic to the Blues," one of the in-depth acoustic guitar courses you get when you subscribe to *The Acoustic Guitar Workshop*. Pick up your old Ovation and check it out at *www.acousticguitarworkshop.com* (April 30, 2009).

6. Special thanks to Allen Arnn, Mosaic's associate pastor of ministry development and director of children's ministries, for his help in writing the section "What about Children's Ministry?"

7. Special thanks to Amos Gray, a former student ministries pastor at Mosaic, for his help in writing the section "What about Student Ministry?"

CHAPTER 6: ROASTING FOR FLAVOR

1. The Greek word *patria* means "running back to some progenitor, ancestry; a nation or tribe, a group of families, all those who in a given people lay claim to a common origin; family, in a wider sense, nation, people." See *www.studylight.org/lex/grk/view .cgi?number=3965* (March 11, 2009).

2. See *http://motherearthtravel.com/united_states/houston/history .htm* (March 13, 2009).

3. Especially in the United States, where becoming independent and comfortable are inherently valued and are promoted as what is good or best.

4. For more information about Dai Mitsutani's life and stay at Mosaic, see Mark DeYmaz, *Building a Healthy Multi-ethnic Church* (San Francisco: Jossey-Bass/Leadership Network, 2007), 115–17.

CHAPTER 7: HUSKING THE OUTER SHELL

1. Mosaic's conflict norms were adapted from Patrick Lencioni, *The Five Dysfunctions of a Team* (San Francisco: Jossey-Bass, 2002).
2. An excellent resource for conflict resolution: *Peacemaking Principles: Responding to Conflict Biblically*, from Peacemaker Ministries, P.O. Box 81130, Billings, MT 59208, *www.peacemaker .net* (April 14, 2009).
3. To view Mosaic's conflict norms, see appendix 5.

CHAPTER 8: STRANGE BREWS

1. I'm thinking about *This Present Darkness*, a work of fiction in which angels, demons, prayer, and spiritual warfare all play a part in the struggle for control of a local church and citizens living in the small town of Ashton. See *www.amazon.com/This-Present-Darkness-Frank-Peretti/dp/0891073906* (February 2009).
2. See Mark DeYmaz, *Building a Healthy Multi-ethnic Church* (San Francisco: Jossey-Bass/Leadership Network, 2007), 90.
3. I believe that the theme of Ephesians can be stated as "the unity of the local church for the sake of the gospel."
4. Such was the thinking of Abbé Faria as voiced to Edmond Dantes in the film *The Count of Monte Cristo* (Touchstone Pictures/Spyglass Entertainment, 2002).

CONCLUSION

1. David Olson, *The American Church in Crisis* (Grand Rapids, Mich.: Zondervan, 2008), 171.

DR. MARK DEYMAZ is the founding pastor and directional leader of the Mosaic Church of Central Arkansas (*www.mosaicchurch.net*), a multi-ethnic and economically diverse church where men and women from more than thirty nations walk, work, and worship God together as one. A recognized leader in the multi-ethnic church movement, Mark's first book, *Building a Healthy Multi-ethnic Church* (Jossey-Bass/Leadership Network, 2007) was a finalist for a 2008 *Christianity Today* Book of the Year Award and for a Resource of the Year Award sponsored by *Outreach Magazine*. He is a columnist for *Outreach Magazine* and a contributing editor for *Leadership* journal. In addition, Mark posts regularly on his blog at *www.markdeymaz.com*.

In 2004, Mark cofounded Mosaix (*www.mosaix.info*), a relational network dedicated to inspiring unity and diversity in the local church throughout North America and beyond. Today Mosaix is a sister network of the Mosaic Alliance and the Mosaic Global Initiative, both led by Erwin Raphael McManus.

Mark and his wife, Linda, have four children, Zack, Emily, Will, and Kate. Linda is the author of two books, including *Mommy, Please Don't Cry* (Multnomah, 1996), a 2004 Retailer's Choice Nominee providing hope and comfort for parents who grieve the loss of a child.

Mark is a graduate of Liberty University in Lynchburg, Virginia (BS Psychology), Western Seminary in Portland, Oregon (MA Exegetical Theology), and Phoenix Seminary in Phoenix, Arizona (DMin).

DR. HARRY LI has been a campus pastor at Mosaic since 2002. Prior to that, he was an associate professor of electrical engineering at the University of Idaho in Moscow. He is a graduate of the University of Tennessee (BSEE) and the Georgia Institute of

Technology (MSEE, PhDEE). In addition to this book, Harry has written many technical articles and papers, including a bestselling textbook on integrated-circuit design.

Harry is also highly involved with a relational network of pastors in central Arkansas dedicated to bringing spiritual renewal and revival to the area through a citywide movement of prayer.

Harry and his wife, Melanie, reside in Little Rock and have three daughters, Anna, Katie, and Meredith.

Building a Healthy Multi-Ethnic Church

Mandate, Commitments and Practices of a Diverse Congregation

Mark DeYmaz

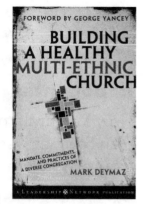

For more than one hundred years, eleven o'clock on Sunday morning has been called the most segregated hour in the land. Despite the integration of public schools, the workplace, and neighborhoods, the local church stubbornly clings to homogeneity. As America grows more and more diverse, the local church will be forced to adapt in order to remain relevant and effective. Good intentions, however, are not enough to inspire systemic change.

Building a Healthy Multi-Ethnic Church explains why the growing fascination with multi-ethnic churches must be focused not on racial reconciliation but on reconciling individuals to Jesus Christ and on reconciling local congregations of faith with the inclusive nature of the New Testament Church.

Through personal stories and a thorough analysis of the biblical text, Mark DeYmaz, pastor of one of the most successful multi-ethnic churches in the country, provides the theological mandate for the multi-ethnic church and outlines seven core commitments required to bring it about. Writing from his comprehensive experience in planting, growing, and encouraging more ethnically diverse communities of faith, he demonstrates why the most effective way to advance the gospel in the twenty-first century will be through strong and vital multi-ethnic churches.

Hardcover: 978-0-7879-9551-5

Exponential

How You and Your Friends Can Start a Missional Church Movement

*Dave Ferguson
and Jon Ferguson*

Exponential communicates a simple strategy that will engage every Christ-follower and challenge every leader to become a reproducing leader, to catalyze a movement that can accomplish Jesus' mission. This book lays out a brief but solid theology for a reproducing strategy and then gives practical how-to's for reproducing Christ-followers, leaders, artists, groups and teams, venues, sites, churches, and networks of churches. Weaved throughout the text is the amazing story of Community Christian Church, started by five friends who used these reproducing strategies to grow one of the most influential churches in the U.S.

Softcover: 978-0-310-32678-6

Exponential Series

AND

The Gathered and Scattered Church

Hugh Halter and Matt Smay

AND helps you—whether you are a mega-church, traditional-church, contemporary-church, or organic-church leader—focus on those who are not moving toward any from of church. Learn how to value existing church forms, while also attracting people to a physical church *and* releasing people into hands-on ministry. *AND* is the very best of the attractional and missional models for church ministry.

Softcover: 978-0-310-32585-7

The Exponential Series is a partnership between Exponential Network, Leadership Network, and Zondervan, featuring several signature books each year to tell the reproducing-church story, to celebrate the diversity of models and approaches God is using to reproduce healthy congregations, and to highlight the innovative practices of healthy reproducing churches.

Leadership Network
Innovation Series

A Multi-Site
Church Roadtrip

Exploring the New Normal

*Geoff Surratt, Greg Ligon,
and Warren Bird*

Hop On for a Guided Tour of the Multi-
Site Church Movement

From multiple locations to internet campuses, the multi-site church movement is changing the shape of the church. What is this rapidly expanding phenomenon all about? Experience the revolution for yourself and see why it has become the "new normal" for growing churches. *A Multi-Site Church Roadtrip* takes you on a tour of multi-site churches across America to see how they're handling the opportunities and challenges raised by this dynamic organizational model.

Travel with tour guides Geoff Surratt, Greg Ligon, and Warren Bird, authors of *The Multi-Site Church Revolution*, on an engaging and humorous journey that shows creative ways churches of all kinds are expanding their impact through multiple locations. Hear the inside stories and learn about the latest developments. Find out firsthand how the churches in this book are broadening their options for evangelism, service, and outreach, while making better use of their ministry funds.

Softcover: 978-0-310-29394-1

Pick up a copy at your favorite bookstore or online!

Sticky Teams

Keeping Your Leadership Team and Staff on the Same Page

Larry Osborne

Serving as a church leader can be a tough assignment. Whatever your role, odds are you've known your share of the frustration, conflict, and disillusionment that come with silly turf battles, conflicting vision, and marathon meetings.

No doubt, you've asked yourself, How did it get this way?

With practical and accessible wisdom, Larry Osborne explains how it got this way. He exposes the hidden roadblocks, structures, and goofy thinking that sabotage even the best-intentioned teams. Then with time-tested and proven strategies, he shows what it takes to get (and keep) a board, staff, and congregation on the same page.

Whatever your situation—from start-up phase, to midsized, to megachurch—Osborne has been there. As the pastor of North Coast Church, he's walked his board, staff, and congregation through the process. Now with warm encouragement and penetrating insights, he shares his secrets to building and maintaining a healthy and unified ministry team that sticks together for the long haul.

Softcover: 978-0-310-32464-5

Pick up a copy at your favorite bookstore or online!

About the Leadership Network Innovation Series

Since 1984, Leadership Network has fostered church innovation and growth by diligently pursuing its far-reaching mission statement: *To identify high-capacity Christian leaders, to connect them with other leaders, and to help them multiply their impact.*

While specific techniques may vary as the church faces new opportunities and challenges, Leadership Network consistently focuses on bringing together entrepreneurial leaders who are pursuing similar ministry initiatives. The resulting peer-to-peer interaction, dialogue, and collaboration—often across denominational lines—helps these leaders better refine their individual strategies and accelerate their own innovations.

To further enhance this process, Leadership Network develops and distributes highly targeted ministry tools and resources, including books, DVDs and videotapes, special reports, e-publications, and free downloads.

Launched in 2006, the Leadership Network Innovation Series presents case studies and insights from leading practitioners and pioneering churches that are successfully navigating the ever-changing streams of spiritual renewal in modern society. Each book offers real stories, about real leaders, in real churches, doing real ministry. Readers gain honest and thorough analyses, transferable principles, and clear guidance on how to put proven ideas to work in their individual settings.

With the assistance of Leadership Network—and the Leadership Network Innovation Series—today's Christian leaders are energized, equipped, inspired, and enabled to multiply their own dynamic kingdom-building initiatives. And the pace of innovative ministry is growing as never before.

For additional information on the mission or activities of Leadership Network, please contact:

L E A D E R S H I P ✖ N E T W O R K
innovation series
800-765-5323
www.leadnet.org
client.care@leadnet.org

Share Your Thoughts

With the Author: Your comments will be forwarded to the author when you send them to *zauthor@zondervan.com*.

With Zondervan: Submit your review of this book by writing to *zreview@zondervan.com*.

Free Online Resources at
www.zondervan.com

Zondervan AuthorTracker: Be notified whenever your favorite authors publish new books, go on tour, or post an update about what's happening in their lives at www.zondervan.com/authortracker.

Daily Bible Verses and Devotions: Enrich your life with daily Bible verses or devotions that help you start every morning focused on God. Visit www.zondervan.com/newsletters.

Free Email Publications: Sign up for newsletters on Christian living, academic resources, church ministry, fiction, children's resources, and more. Visit www.zondervan.com/newsletters.

Zondervan Bible Search: Find and compare Bible passages in a variety of translations at www.zondervanbiblesearch.com.

Other Benefits: Register yourself to receive online benefits like coupons and special offers, or to participate in research.

ZONDERVAN.com/
AUTHORTRACKER
follow your favorite authors